THE ORIGIN OF OUR RITUALS

A Question & Answer Guide
To Rediscovering Our Catholic Heritage

AuthorHouse™
1663 Liberty Drive
Bloomington, IN 47403
www.authorhouse.com
Phone: 1-800-839-8640

All biblical extracts have been taken from the New American Bible (NAB) unless otherwise noted.

Published by AuthorHouse   05/02/2013
Library of Congress Catalogue-in-Publication Data is available upon request.

ISBN: 978-1-4817-2492-0 (sc)
ISBN: 978-1-4817-2493-7 (e)

I dedicate this book to a dear friend from Lexington, Kentucky, who inspired me to be grateful to God, Mr. Harry Cloud McKenna.

TABLE OF CONTENTS

INTRODUCTION

QUESTION:

WHY DID I WRITE A Reference Guide About The Origin Of Our Rituals?

BRIEF ANSWER:
Nothing we do, say or hear in Church is by chance. We need to know the reasons and origins of our rituals in order to appreciate our heritage.

SCRIPTURE:
John 4:26
John 2:1
Romans 1:20
Acts 2:41

LEARN MORE: My parents never went to church when I was young. My dad was agnostic, and my mom was a non-practicing Catholic. When I was about eight years old, my grandma Adela started taking me to early Mass. I well remember that Sunday morning when she reminded me to stay quiet as we rushed into church. I got quite upset. *"How come only the fellow in funny robes gets to talk all the time?"* I asked. My little mind wondered as I looked up at the statues. When I heard the prayer "Our Father", I jumped for joy because I knew that we were almost at the end of Mass and getting ready to go home.

By the time that I was 15, my mom had experienced a conversion and become a fervent Catholic. As part of my rebellion against my parents, I began to attend a nondenominational church that my aunt and cousins frequented. One Sunday morning as I was getting ready to attend service there, my mom came into my room and asked me *"Where do you think you're going?"* I looked at her through the mirror. *"To church"*, I said. She replied, *"No you're not, you are coming with me to Mass"*. I squinted at her. "Mass? Mass is boring". To my mind a Protestant service was more fun, the music was upbeat and the people came out to greet each other. For my own safety though I did go to Mass with mom that day. I trudged on to church, hating every step.

About six months later, noticing my rudderless unease, a friend invited me to attend a youth pizza night at the local parish. It was there that I learned the Truth of the Eucharist.

That evening when the Priest told us that Jesus was Truly Present in the white round wafer I thought it was a joke at first. Then I pondered, *"Jesus is God. If Jesus is able to transform Water into Wine, why can't He transform the Wafer into His Own Self?"* (John 2:1) That night as I lay in bed I had my first serious conversation with God.

How to use this guide? I encourage you to browse the Table of Contents and start at any page. If you are interested in the symbolic nature of what we say, do, and see in church you may enjoy the first two chapters, "On Entering Church" and "As Mass Begins". If you are looking for a deeper theological meaning, I encourage you to read the last chapter "As We Go Forth." Capitalized words in the middle of sentences stress key concepts. To learn more, refer to the INDEX at the end of the book. If you see a number at the end of a paragraph, it refers to the number on the Notes page. I hope this helps you appreciate our 2000 years of heritage. Many blessings!

Part One

ON ENTERING CHURCH

QUESTION:

WHY DO WE See A Double Door At The Entrance Of Church?

BRIEF ANSWER:

These doors or portals represent Jesus the gateway into eternal life. [1]

SCRIPTURE:
John 10:9
John 14:6
Acts 4:12

LEARN MORE: Before 325 AD, many churches in Rome had previously been temples dedicated to pagan deities. [278] The Emperor Constantine donated many of these buildings to Christianity.[2] These structures had a center double door called the Royal Gate Door, with two smaller double doors on each side. The Royal Door was well ornamented. [3]

The Church found fresh symbolism in this for their house of worship. [4] Jesus is the only door into Heaven. One set of side double doors signified the entrance for the triumphant Church in Heaven made up of saints departed. The other set was for the Church purging their sins in Purgatory. [5] The Royal Gate Door was reserved for the pilgrim Church on earth, represented by each of us.

The Gospel of John teaches us that Jesus called himself the gate and that whoever enters through him shall be saved. [6] Bishop Ignatius of Antioch wrote in this same vein in c107 AD. [7]

"Jesus Christ is the door of the Father, through which enter Abraham, the prophets, the apostles and the church."

WHY DO WE Bless Ourselves With Holy Water?

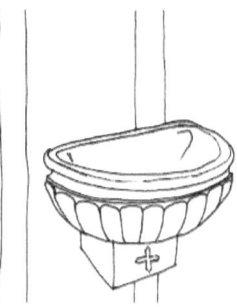

God uses water to purify us as we are reminded of our Baptism.

Matthew 3:16
Numbers 5:17
Acts 1:5

Baptism means "Immersion" in Greek. For us, it signifies new birth into the family of God and into His Church. This is no ordinary ritual. After Jesus' resurrection c29 AD, His disciples waited for Pentecost, the day that God the Holy Spirit came to baptize them. They, in turn, baptized converts by immersing them in rivers or pools. From then on, before praying, Christians washed their faces and hands with the holy water that had been blessed on Sunday. This reminded them of their Baptism. [262]

After the Roman Empire accepted Christianity in 313 AD, all entrances to churches were equipped with pools and baths that came to be known as Baptismal Founts. [8] Those who wished to follow Christ as their savior had first to be purified by these waters. [9] These converts, known as Catechumens, were immersed in pools shaped like a cross with flowing waters..[10] As soon as they emerged, Christians ran up to the fountain with their containers to collect this water considered holy. Many kept it in their homes for blessing themselves. [11]

As early as the 11th Century, smaller founts at church entrances had become common. When people came inside church, they touched this Holy Water, for no one was to come inside the Lord's house with an unclean spirit. Some of these stoups were reserved for poor and laboring people. Others were for the nobility. Today, we all share the same Holy Water Founts to remind us of our unity through our Baptism. [12]

WHY DO WE Genuflect In Church?

We show our humble disposition before God.

Psalm 95:6
Philippians 2:10
Romans 14:11
Ephesians 3:14

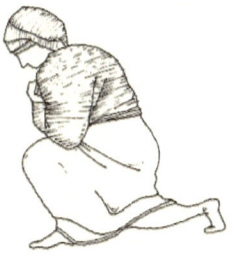

In 328 BC, Alexander the Great ordered his armies to genuflect before him on their left knee after defeating his enemies in battle. [13] Emperors of Rome demanded the same respect every time a senator came into their presence. [14]

The Church adopted the same genuflecting pattern of reverence and submission to God alone. Therefore, we bend the right knee instead of the left before Christ, present in the Eucharist.[15]

During the 5th Century, Christians genuflected before receiving the Body and Blood of Christ in Holy Communion. By the 9th Century, they also genuflected in front of the Book of Gospels displayed on the altar. In 1264 AD, the Church promoted genuflection before the tabernacle, or if the Eucharist was exposed in the monstrance for Adoration. Every Christmas and March 25 at the feast of the Annunciation, we genuflect during the recitation of the Creed when *"Jesus was incarnate of the Virgin Mary and became man"*.

WHY DO WE Have Depictions of Saints?

They are present among us, their lives inspire us and their prayers aid us. We don't worship them we venerate them.

Exodus 20:4
Exodus 25:18
1 Corinthians 13:12

Since 2nd Century, the Church has called all its members Saints. [291] This is because the Sacraments of Baptism and the Eucharist unite us all. This is also why the Church calls itself the Communion of Saints. In those early days, the Church still looked up to Christ as the only one to whom to pray. When one of the Saints died as a Martyr for Christ, their body was laid to rest in a special place where people came to touch the tomb and celebrate Mass. [270] Soon these places became shrines, and eventually churches. On its walls were paintings or mosaics depicting the life of its Saint, and other biblical scenes.

Roman artists who worshiped the emperors painted them wearing golden sun disks round their heads. In the 5th Century, Christians adopted this use of the halo for their saints and Christ. [16]

By 432 AD, the Church of Santa Maria Maggiore in Rome had painted stories on the walls that depicted the childhood of Jesus and His Blessed Mother. [76] Bishops discovered that decorating these temples with beautiful color pictures helped people to Pray, and aided those who could not read to understand Scripture and their Faith. Icons of saints also became popular. [77]

Around 540 AD, Bishop Gregory of Tours introduced colored glass in churches. [271] By the 12th Century, this new form of art inspired artists to depict the Saints in stained glass windows. These saints reflect the light that comes from God. [17]

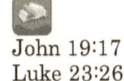 **WHY DO WE See The Stations Of The Cross?**

✔️ We contemplate the suffering Jesus so we can grow in our Faith. [18]

John 19:17
Luke 23:26

A Station of the Cross is a depiction of one of the stages along Jesus' journey towards His crucifixion in Jerusalem. The fourteen low relief paintings that you see on the walls of churches, are called the Stations of the Cross, also known as the "*Via Crucis*".

The Church calls them *Stations* because they are meant to be points at which we stop and meditate, as if we are on a mini pilgrimage through Jerusalem.

This devotion originated in 460 AD. Bishop Petronius from Bologna built a series of interconnected chapels in the monastery of Santo Stefano. Each of these chapels represented Jerusalem's most important shrines relating to the life and crucifixion of our Lord Jesus. His parishioners could relive the Passion of our Lord by visiting these Stations and contemplating Jesus' sufferings. Later, the Church adopted a simplified form of these chapel Stations and incorporated them as murals or paintings on walls for every parish church. In 1730, Pope Clement XII fixed the number of Stations to fourteen. [19]

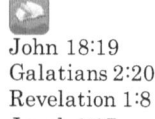 **WHY DO WE See Symbols In Church, And What Do They Mean?**

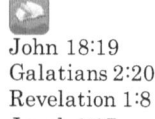 They point us to important Faith teachings.

John 18:19
Galatians 2:20
Revelation 1:8
Jonah 1:17

After 29 AD, when Christians travelled to foreign lands, they brought their symbols with them to remind each other of the Truths of their Faith. For example, a fish depicts Jesus carrying us in His belly through the stormy waters of life. This symbol of a fish also represents an acronym. The word Fish in Greek is "*ICHTHUS*". Each letter stands for "*Jesus Christ, Son of God, Savior*". [295]

In 250 AD, the Alpha and Omega symbols became popular among Christians because they signified Christ as the Beginning and the End of Everything. [301] They also formed a monogram of the Name of Jesus by using the first three letters of His Name in Greek "*I-H-S*". His name carried power against Satan.

In 314 AD, the Emperor Constantine painted a "*Chi-Rho*" on his soldier's shields, consisting of the two initials for Christ "X-*P*", in order to signify victory.

When artists began to depict the crucifixion of Christ, they added to the Cross four letters in Latin, "*I-N-R-I*" which stand for "*Jesus of Nazareth King of the Jews*".

The most common symbol found in Catacombs of the 3rd Century is the Cross or Anchor, the symbol of our Salvation and Hope. If the Cross has Jesus' corpus on it is a Crucifix. By the 5th Century AD, Churches had a tall Crucifix above the Sanctuary known as the Rood. Jesus was shown as triumphant over pain and sin. [20]

WHY DO WE See Three Vases With Oils?

They are used for God's anointing, healing, and blessing.

James 5:14
1 Kings 1:39
1 Kings 19:15

The three Holy Oils are kept in a prominent place in Church called Ambry. The Oil of Catechumens is use to anoint those preparing for Baptism. The Oil of Chrism is also used for Baptism, as well as Confirmation, Ordination and Blessing of new Altars. 21 The Oil of the Sick is used for the Anointing of the Sick. The vases are called the Ampullae or Chrismals. 22

During the 2nd Century, Bishops blessed these Oils during the Vigil Mass of Holy Thursday. The Bishop himself mixed the Oils with Balsam while the Deacons held the different vases. After the Blessing, the newly Baptized were anointed with the Oil of Catechumens, which was to give God's seal; then the Oil of Chrism that was to grant the gift of the Holy Spirit. 23

The Bible tells us in the Book of James, how Christ's ministers anointed the sick with the Oil of the Sick in order to heal them from their infirmities. In fact, many Christians were used to Jewish physicians who anointed the ill with olive oil mixed with wines in the hope for a prompt recovery. By the 3rd Century, this Oil of the Sick was also used for Exorcisms. 296

After a person was anointed with the Holy Oils, only a blessed comb could touch its hair, called the Pecten. Priests and clerics of the 6th Century before administering the Sacraments they combed their hair with a blessed comb known as the "*Pecten Consecrationis*". This holy object reminded them of their Consecration to God with the Oil of Chrism. 299

WHY DO WE Have A Sanctuary?

This holy space sets the boundaries inside Church for God's Sacrifice and His Scripture Proclamation.

Exodus 25:8
1 Chronicles 22:19

The Sanctuary is the elevated place where the Altar stands. This place is known as the Holy of Holies reserved for the Sacrifice of Jesus on the Cross and His proclamation of His Word. Sanctuary derives from the Latin, "*Sanctus*" meaning holy or separated from the ordinary. The word Saint comes down to us from this word. [24]

For the First Century Jews, Sanctuary was a sacred space in the Temple separated by a 60-foot tall veil curtain where only the high priest could enter once a year on behalf of the people. [25]

Christians of the 2nd Century borrowed the term "*Sanctuary*" to define a place where members of the Faithful had been martyred and this became known as a shrine dedicated to their Memory. In 320 AD "*Sanctuary*" took another meaning as the elevated platform in the Apse of a Basilica upon which the Altar stood. After 800 AD, a criminal who stood on the steps of a Sanctuary was immune from arrest. This meaning is used today when we speak about an animal or bird sanctuary as a place where they are protected. During Mass, only Ministers may stand inside the Sanctuary.

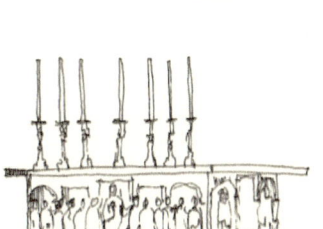

WHY DO WE Bow Before The Altar?

We revere and adore Jesus on His Cross, which is the Altar. Bowing is a sign of humility.

Luke 23:39
Luke 24:25
Revelation 6:9
Exodus 27:1

In 458 BC, prisoners of war bowed down before the Roman Dictator Cincinnatus. They lowered their body to look small and show submission. [289]

Jesus, in the year 29 AD, began His Sacrifice on a Table at the Last Supper and completed it on a Bloody Cross. His Cross became his Altar. [26] Noah was the first person we know of, who built an Altar to God. For ancient cultures, an Altar was a stone structure built for the slaughter of animals offered as gifts to the gods.

In the 2nd Century, wood was the material of choice for Christian Altars. This was because they needed to be portable for as long as Masses were said in Catacombs. The wooden planks were placed on top of Martyrs' Graves. [27] Wood decays, however, and better materials were needed for Altars as the Church became established.

The first person to describe the Altar as the Table of the Lord was Pope Sixtus II in 257 AD. In 364 AD, St. Optatus of Milevi called the Altar the "*Wood*" and "*Cross of Christ.*" [28] Around 361 AD, St Hilary presented several Altars made of silver to the Church at Rome. Following the Council of Epeaune in France, in 517 AD, all Altars were made of Stone in order to be permanent. [29]

Today an Altar may be made of either wood or stone as long as it is permanently installed. [30] If, for some reason, the altar is not permanent it should have a blessed square stone, which is taken out when not in use.

WHAT ARE Relics? Do All Altars Have Them?

Relics are objects that belonged to or touched a Martyr or Saint. If possible, all Altars should have relics.

Acts 8:54
Revelation 6:9

A Reliquary is a small cylindrical vessel containing the Relic of a Saint for our veneration. The moment after St Peter was crucified upside down in Rome in c64 AD, people began to venerate all the Martyrs and care for their graves. They soon collected their belongings such as clothing items and even dried bones from their bodies, which were used to heal people's infirmities. [31]

In 313 AD, the Emperor Constantine subsidized 25 public Roman buildings to become Churches. Each new church adopted a Saint or Martyr as their protector. [32] A relic of this Patron Saint, or another Saint, was placed inside the Altar stone or under the Altar. This ritual had a Biblical root since the Book of Revelation sees the figures of the Saintly Martyrs under the Altar. [33] This tradition continued until 1965. Since then, the Church recommends but does not prescribe, the use of relics in Altars. [34]

An Altar is so significant that it is consecrated with blessings and Chrism Oils that echo our Baptism. This dedication makes every Altar Sacred. Relics may enhance an Altar. However, they do not make it Holy, in themselves.

WHY DO WE Have More Than One Altar In Church?

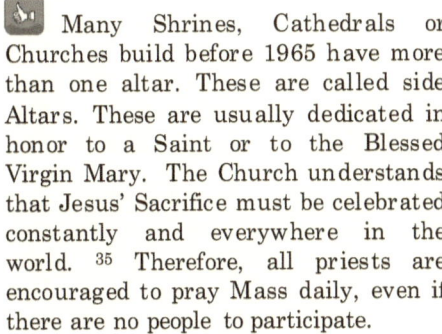 Many Shrines, Cathedrals or Churches build before 1965 have more than one altar. These are called side Altars. These are usually dedicated in honor to a Saint or to the Blessed Virgin Mary. The Church understands that Jesus' Sacrifice must be celebrated constantly and everywhere in the world. [35] Therefore, all priests are encouraged to pray Mass daily, even if there are no people to participate.

✓ Priests are encouraged to pray Mass daily, even if it is in private.

🔄 Exodus 20:24
Hebrews 9:12
Malachi 1:11

During the 6th Century, with the election of Pope Gregory I as the first Monk to become a Pope, Monasticism became popular. [36] The subsequent increase in the number of Priests who were Monks created a demand for side Altars. [37] Each Priest celebrated his private Mass in silence as the Community attended Mass in the main nave of the Church. [38] During this time the concept of a Votive Mass became popular. A priest was asked to pray his daily Mass for one particular intention. As the demand for Votive Masses increased, the demand for side Altars also increased. [39]

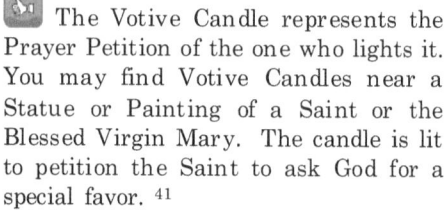

WHY DO WE See Candles Lit In Church?

It's the symbol for Christ the Light of the World. There are four types of candles. 40

John 8:12
John 12:46
Acts 20:8
Isaiah 9:1

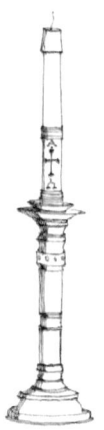

The Votive Candle represents the Prayer Petition of the one who lights it. You may find Votive Candles near a Statue or Painting of a Saint or the Blessed Virgin Mary. The candle is lit to petition the Saint to ask God for a special favor. 41

The second type is the Altar Candle. There are six of these, three at each end of the Altar. All six Candles burn on Feast Days and Holy Days of Obligation, such as Christmas and Easter. 42 On Sundays, only four of them are lit, and for Weekday Masses just two. 43 A seven candle is lit in a cathedral basilica when the local archbishop celebrates Mass. 297

The third type is the Procession Candle. Two of these large Candles accompany the Crucifix and the Book of Gospels in processions.

Last, a tall, engraved Paschal Candle burns only during Easter, Funerals and Baptisms. This Paschal Candle represents the Resurrection of Christ. All other Candles used in Mass receive their light from it at Easter Vigil Mass. 44

The tradition of lighting Candles originated during Jesus' first Mass at the Last Supper in the Upper Room. 45 After His Resurrection in c29 AD, the Church continued to gather in the evenings for Mass and the Candles symbolized Christ the Light shining in the darkness. 46

WHY DO WE Have A Sacristy?

It stores the sacred vessels and vestments, and provides a place for Ministers to prayerfully prepare for Holy Mass.

2 Kings 10:22
Leviticus 16:24

Sacristy comes from the Latin word "Secretarium" which means a place set aside for purposes of secrecy. Secrecy was particularly important for the early Church because from the 4th Century onwards no town was unaffected by invasions of foreign tribes looting treasures. The first places where barbarians looked for gold and silver were Churches and public buildings. 47

Christians built two locked rooms to secure their Sacred Treasures inside their Churches. One of these was called the Diaconicon, and the other the Prothesis. Important writings like the Book of Gospels and the Lectionary, as well as Relics and Vestments, were kept safe within the Diaconicon. Sacred Vessels like the Chalice, the Ciborium, the Paten, and, above all, the Pyx containing the Body of Christ in the Eucharist were kept in the Prothesis. 48

In 565 AD, Emperor Justin II ordered Churches to build their Sacristies into two separate Apses to the east of the Sanctuary. Since the 16th Century, these two rooms have become one again, and today we call this room the Sacristy. 49

WHY DO
WE See
Deacons In
Church?

 Deacons
are Ministers
Ordained to
assist at Mass
and preach the
Word of God.

Acts 6:1
1 Timothy 3:8
Romans 16:1
Philippians 1:1

"Deacon" comes from the Greek word *"Diakonos"* meaning servant or runner. Deacons have three roles in the Church since the second century. First, a Deacon is the Servant at the Table who helps at Mass. A Deacon leads the Congregation into Song and Prayer. Second, a Deacon is the Servant of the Word. He may Proclaim the Readings and Preach a Homily. Third, a Deacon is also the Servant of Charity. His role in ancient times included guarding Church doors against the Persecution of Christians. Later, Deacons visited the sick, the elderly, and the poor to distribute alms and food. Around the year 42 AD, The Bible tells us that St Stephen was the first Deacon to become a Martyr for the Faith. [75]

The *"Didascalia Apostolorum"* is the earliest document referring to the Ordination of Deacons and dates back to c250 AD. Around 314 AD, Pope Sylvester I introduced a Croatian long tunic with wide sleeves called a Dalmatic for Deacons, and Bishops to wear during Mass. [50]

Only a Bishop may ordain a Deacon. Permanent Deacons may be married and have a family, but if their spouse dies they must remain celibate thereafter. Transitional Deacons are called Seminarians. They are ordained to the Diaconate before they receive their Priesthood, also from a Bishop. [51]

WHY DO WE See Bishops Or Priests?

Every priest at Mass represents his bishop and acts in the person of Jesus Christ. A Bishop is a priest successor of the first Apostles.

Luke 22:19
Matthew 28:19
Acts 3:6
Acts 9:17
Acts 9:34

The Bishop is a Priest ordained by another Bishop. He represents the line of Succession from the Apostles appointed by Christ. [267] Priests are ministers ordained to offer the Sacraments. [52] When we follow the Line of Succession back to 29 AD, we go back to Christ, the First Priest.

In the 2nd Century, there were no Parish Churches. Christians met in private homes. As their number grew, they might buy a house for worship in their town. This property was owned in a trust. The person in whose name the house was registered was the custodian, or "*Episkopos*" in Greek for Bishop. [53]

The Bishop was the only person who had the right to Celebrate the Eucharistic Sacrifice. This was because the Twelve Apostles had received the Authority from Jesus "*Do so in Memory of Me*". [54] The group of men who accompanied the Bishop were called Elders, or in Greek "*Presbuteroi*", from which the term Presbyter or Priest comes.

As the Church expanded, Bishops delegated the Celebration of the Mass to their Elders by the Laying on of Hands, and through Anointing them with Holy Oils. This Act became the Sacrament of Ordination, or Holy Orders. By 215 AD, the Church had a codified ritual of the Ordination of Men to Priesthood documented in the Apostolic Tradition of Bishop Hippolytus of Rome. [55] Whenever we see a priest praying Mass, he is representing his Bishop. [101]

WHY DO WE See A Bishop Wear A Miter?

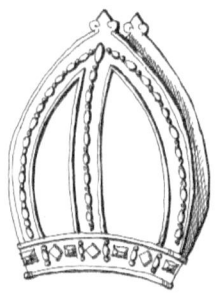

It's a symbol of their belonging to God and having authority to teach, preach and sanctify.

Exodus 28:39
Exodus 29:6
Colossians 1:18

"Miter" is a Greek word meaning Headband or Turban. The Miter has its origins in Judaism, where the High Priest would wear a tall headpiece to symbolize that he belonged to God Who is Holy. Also by wearing the Miter, he could compensate for any mistakes during his worship since God's Holiness was upon his head. [56]

The Bishops of the 4th Century adopted a folding, triangular shaped cap symbol of the Blessed Trinity, in order to stand out amidst the crowds during Liturgical Celebrations and as a symbol of Christ's Authority to Teach, Preach and Sanctify God's People. [57]

Since the 16th Century, the Bishop uses a slightly differently shaped Miter with more curvy sides, symbol of the tongues of fire. He wears it while processing at Mass, and at other times when acting in Authority such as when preaching a Sermon. [58]

If more than one Bishop is at Mass, the main Celebrant wears a precious ornamented Miter while the Concelebrants only use a simple white one. During Mass, The Miter Server holds the Bishop's Miter with a shawl-like veil called a Vimpa. [59]

When a Bishop wears a Miter, this reminds him and us that he is representing Christ, the Head of the Church.

WHY DO WE See A Bishop Wear A Zucchetto?

This cap reminds clerics of their humble submission to God alone and freedom from slavery of sin.

2 Samuel 15:30
Esther 6:12
Numbers 6:18
Acts 2:47
1 Corinthians 11:7

The Pope wears a white Pileolus or Zucchetto also known as a Solideo cap. A Cardinal wears a red Zuchetto, a Bishop wears a purple one while Priests may wear black ones, all as symbols for their servant hood to God.

Solideo comes from the Latin phrase *"Soli Deo Gloria"* meaning "Glory to God Alone." *"Zucchetto"* in Italian means *small* or *hard head*, the same origin of the word zucchini. For centuries before the Christian era, Greeks and Romans shaved the heads of all their conquered subjects as a badge of slavery. A Pileolus cap was placed on the shaved head of a former slave upon receiving freedom. [60]

During the latter part of the 5th Century, Monks began to shave the tops of their heads as signs of their servant hood, and their giving of Glory to God alone. Then Clerics began to use a Zucchetto cap as a sign of their freedom from sin and to protect their heads from the cold. By the 13th Century, the Zucchetto or Solideo cap was officially worn by all the Clerics to signify they were the servants of the servants of God. [61] Today, the Bishop removes his Solideo during the Eucharistic Prayer, as a sign of respect for the Sacrament about to take place. [62]

 WHY DO WE See Priests Wear Clerical Collars?

It's a symbol for living a life of dedication to God and Church.

Romans 13:14
Romans 4:12
Acts 1:26

When a Cleric wears his vestments in Church, he does this to represent his people before God in the best possible way. When he wears his Clerical Collar outside of Mass, he best represents God to his people. Cleric is a Greek word meaning Heritage. [267]

Bishops and Priests did not wear any distinctive garments outside of Mass until 675 AD, when the Stole was prescribed as their badge at the Synod of Braga. The white Clerical Collar became part of Priestly Dress around 1700 AD, when a white lapel on the collar came to signify a priest's commitment to God and Church, much like a wedding ring. As the Priest dresses for Mass, he disappears as an individual in order to let Christ Appear. He covers his Clerical Collar. If the Alb is too small to do this fully, then he must wear a rectangular piece of linen around his neck secured with long tapes attached at two corners. This cloth is called the Amice. [63]

During the first centuries, married men were chosen as Bishops. [78] In the Eastern Rite of the Catholic Church, married men may be ordained as Deacons and Priests but not as Bishops. In the Western Rite, men freely choose Celibacy in response to a call from God to have their hearts and minds centered on God and His Church.[266] A man in both the East and the West who has already received the Sacrament of Holy Orders may no longer marry. [64]

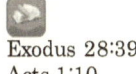 WHY DO
WE See
Priests And
Ministers
Wear An Alb?

✓ It signifies a life of purity and grace received at Baptism.

Exodus 28:39
Acts 1:10

In Latin "*Alba*" means White, and this color was always identified with Purity. During the 1st Century, the Alb was part of Jewish priestly vestments at the Temple. Jesus and his disciples wore a white, pure linen garment at the Seder Meal or Last Supper of c29 AD.[263] During this time, Roman men of the noble class, including senators, wore white toga-like vestments with sleeves, called "*Alba Romana*", at ceremonies. [65]

The Church adopted the "*Alba Romana*" as the symbol of God's Grace given freely to each Person at Baptism. Whether the newly baptized person was a Roman citizen, a free person or a slave, all Baptized People received their "*Alba Romana*" during the Easter Vigil Mass. In 398 AD, at the Four Synod of Carthage, the Bishops prescribed the Alb for all clerics to use in Mass. [300]

Today, we see Altar Servers, Deacons, Priests and other Ministers wearing an Alb at Mass, to remind them of their baptism and to purify their lives as they stand before their Crucified and Risen Lord.[66]

 **WHY DO WE See Priests And Deacons Wear Stoles?**

 This is a symbol of authority, as God's yoke is placed over the heads of Ministers who till the soil in His vineyard, the Church.

Mark 16:14
Exodus 29:43

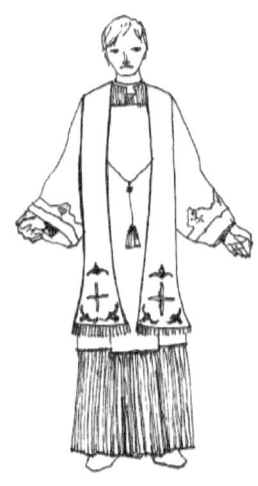

 The word "*Stole*" comes from the Greek word meaning Dress. Roman women of the 1st Century wore a stole over their tunics. Bishops of the 2nd Century adopted a simplified form of this scarf-like apparel as their symbol of Service and Authority. [67] In 177 AD, Bishop St Ireneus described the passing on of Christ's authority to His Apostles, "*The Apostles in turn left Bishops as their successors*". [68] As they passed their authority over to them, they also passed on the tradition of wearing Stoles. A 4th Century manuscript at the Bavarian State Library depicts a Bishop Baptizing a man while wearing a Stole. [69]

During the Synod of Braga in Portugal, in 675 AD, the Stole was prescribed for all Priests. Previously, the Stole had only been required for Deacons, who wore them across their left shoulders.

During the 9th Century AD, all Priests who traveled had to wear a Stole as their priestly identity badge. Every Stole had a Cross in the center, which the Minister kissed before assuming it. This ritual reminded them of their delegated authority received from Christ upon the Cross. After that, the Minister Prayed. [70]

"*Lord, restore the Stole of Immortality, which I lost through the collusion of our first parents. And, unworthy as I am to approach Thy sacred Mysteries, may I yet gain Eternal joy*".

Priests wear the Stole under their Chasuble.

WHY DO WE See A Priest Wear A Cincture?

It reminds them to be vigilant, to have spiritual alertness and purity.

John 21:18
Exodus 28:39
Mark 13:32

The Word Cincture comes from the Latin *"Cingulum"* meaning Belt. Its origin comes from the Jewish Temple of 832 BC, where only the high priest was allowed to enter the Holy of Holies through curtains three feet thick. A rope was tied to him in case God stroke him dead, so people might pull his body out, for no one could step inside the Sanctuary room. [279]

The Church did not adopt this item as part of liturgical garments right away. In 600 AD, Irish Bishops and Priests were the first to wear a common Celtic girdle around their tunics to confine their loose Albs and give them greater freedom of movement. Their Deacons, though, would wear their Albs without a Cincture. Around the 9th Century, the Church of Rome decided to adopt the Irish tradition of wearing the "Cingulum" as part of their liturgical attire. That long Cincture was made of hemp ornamented with pieces of silk, it was folded in half, wrapped around the waist, then slipped the knotted ends through the loop and tightened around the waist. It was donned during the recitation of the prayer. [71]

"Gird me, O Lord, with the Girdle of Purity".

WHY DO WE See A Priest Wear A Chasuble?

The Chasuble is the symbol for Jesus' unconditional love. When a Priest dons it, he is reminded to give his life for every one of his Parishioners

Exodus 28:6
2 Timothy 4:13

"*Chasuble*" in Latin means little tent or house. Around 1400 BC, during prayer, the Israelites wore a shawl called in Hebrew, "*Tallith*" or little tent. This garment was worn over their heads and symbolized the presence of God. In the same way, that God dwelled inside a large tent or Tabernacle. This became the origin of the Chasuble.

By the 1st Century AD, distinguished Roman men wore short hooded capes or Chasubles when attending public services. This was no ordinary garment though. Only Citizens of Rome could wear a Chasuble because it signified their social level ranked according to the properties they owned.

We know that Saint Paul owned one and that he died a martyr wearing it. There were two ways that 1st Century Romans executed people. Those who were not Citizens were thrown to wild beasts or crucified. Citizens like St Paul were beheaded instead while wearing their Chasubles. 72

The Church adopted the garment for use in Mass to emphasize that this was no ordinary activity. 268 A Christian Chasuble was made of silk and had sleeves and ornaments. During the 6th Century, the Chasuble became the norm for all Clergy celebrating Mass. The only exception was that its length and square cut-down shape was increased. Deacons at Mass wear a Chasuble-like vestment called the Dalmatic. 73

 WHY DO WE See The Priestly Chasuble In Different Colors?

They represent the various stages of Jesus' Life thus different Liturgical Seasons and Feasts.

Leviticus 8:5

In Northern Italy and France around 800 AD the People began to use different colors to better mark each epoch of Jesus' ministry and life in their calendars. By the 12th Century, all Churches had adopted four basic colors.

Red represents Fire and appears on Feast Days of the Holy Spirit, the Passion of Our Lord, Feasts of Holy Martyrs and Funeral Masses. [74]

White represents Light and appears at Christmas, Easter, Feasts of the Virgin Mary and other Virgin Saints.

Purple signifies Royalty, and appears at Advent and Lent because these two periods are where Jesus manifests His Kingship most.

Green is for growth. The Church uses it during all other times of the Christian year.

Additional colors were added throughout the Centuries such as Blue during Feast Days for the Blessed Virgin Mary. Gold instead of White used by the Holy Father and his Bishops. Pink as a symbol of anticipation that something good is about to happen. Pink was used for the Second or Fourth Sunday in Lent, known as Gaudete Sunday and Laetare Sunday respectively.

Part Two

AS MASS BEGINS

? WHY DO WE See Ministers And Priests Processing Into Church?

✓ It reminds us that we are a pilgrim people and Jesus leads us triumphantly to Heaven.

Mark 11:7
Psalm 122:1
Joshua 6:4
1 Peter 2:6

After Constantine had accepted Christianity in 313 AD, he donated 25 large public buildings called basilicas to the Church. At that time, the Romans were famous for triumphant parades that celebrated newly conquered territories, where slaves and Priests led the way carrying incense with the Emperor following in the rear. [79]

Since then, Christians borrowed this pagan tradition and have welcomed Christ the King and His Ministers every Sunday into Church. [80] In a similar way, they approach the Altar in a procession reminiscent of Roman Parades.

The first to enter is a Server called the Thurifer bearing Incense. Next is the Cross Bearer holding a large Crucifix, with an Altar Server on either side each holding a large Candle.[81] A Deacon or a Lector follows, carrying the Book of Gospels overhead in triumph. Next are Concelebrant Priests. Finally, the Bishop follows with his Scepter as a Symbol of God's Authority, with the Miter Server and the Crosier Bearer both wearing a Vimpa, bringing up the rear. [82] From the moment that the Priest or Bishop begins this procession, they no longer represent themselves. [83] They represent Christ the King. This is why they and their servers follow last. [84] At the end of Mass, they will process in the same form and we call this moment the Recessional.

WHY DO WE Sing In Church?

✅ This is our communal jubilation for we have been baptized.

Mark 14:26
Ephesians 5:19
Colossians 3:16
Psalm 96:11
Psalm 100:4

It is through song that we reach the heart. It is through language that we reach the mind. St Augustine said, "*Who sings prays twice*". [85] Singing is proven to shift our conscious mind by triggering memories, postures, emotions that elevates us to a spiritual realm. [302]

At His First Mass in c29 AD, Jesus and his disciples sang Psalms and Hymns of Praise to God as they remembered the original Passover Meal. In the same way, the Church prays in Song as we recall Christ's Passover Meal and Sacrifice in the Mass. The Christians of the first four centuries didn't have musical instruments, only their voices and their joy of the Resurrection. [86] They knew that song was not to please others around them, but to pray and praise their God. [87] That jubilation continued throughout the centuries. As both affluent and penniless people pulled stone carts to build their Cathedrals, they all sang hymns of praise to God.

 WHY DO WE See Priests Kiss The Altar?

✓ He is Greeting Jesus on our behalf.

Matthew 26:49
Luke 7:38

Kissing the Altar is one of Four Rituals surviving from the Original Mass of 150 AD. Kissing is the blending of two souls into one. The Altar represents the Cross of Christ. By Kissing It, the Minister greets Jesus and blends his soul with His Soul. Because, by a kiss from Judas, Jesus was condemned to death, so, by a new kiss, we reconcile and show Him our deep love.

The Priest also Kisses the Altar at the end of Mass to give thanks unto God, who has counted him worthy of such great mysteries. [88]

Christianity took root in Mediterranean society. In that culture, a kiss was more than a romantic gesture because the Mediterranean people believed their souls lived in their breath. By giving someone else a kiss, this signified the sharing of their spirits. In 350 AD, St Cyril of Jerusalem, reflecting on the suffering Jesus, noticed that true love always required a price. By dying on the Cross, Jesus gave us all a Kiss. By kissing the Altar, we show Him that we are grateful. He wrote, *"The kiss is also reconciliation, and so it is holy"* [89]

God does need not our bowing down or kissing though. We do this only because it reminds us of who God is in our lives.

WHY DO WE Make The Sign Of The Cross?

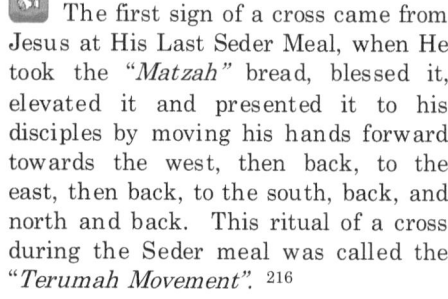 This sign links us back to our Baptism and reminds us that we are royal people. [97]

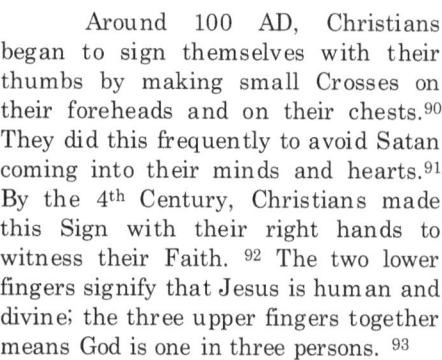
Matthew 28:19
Exodus 29:27

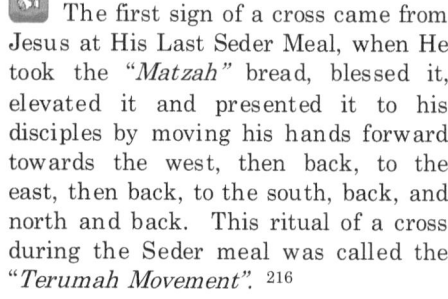 The first sign of a cross came from Jesus at His Last Seder Meal, when He took the *"Matzah"* bread, blessed it, elevated it and presented it to his disciples by moving his hands forward towards the west, then back, to the east, then back, to the south, back, and north and back. This ritual of a cross during the Seder meal was called the *"Terumah Movement"*. [216]

Around 100 AD, Christians began to sign themselves with their thumbs by making small Crosses on their foreheads and on their chests.[90] They did this frequently to avoid Satan coming into their minds and hearts.[91] By the 4th Century, Christians made this Sign with their right hands to witness their Faith. [92] The two lower fingers signify that Jesus is human and divine; the three upper fingers together means God is one in three persons. [93]

By 407 AD, Christians, had begun tracing a Symbol of the Cross over their bodies before Mass, just as we do today, and adding *"In the name of the Father, the Son and the Holy Ghost"*. [94] For these Christians the touch to the forehead signified Jesus coming down from the Father. [95] The touch to the chest signified Jesus becoming Human. The touch on the left shoulder signified Jesus descending into hell by His Death. And the touch on the right shoulder signified His Glorious Ascension to the Father's Right Side in Heaven. [96]

WHY DO WE Hear The Greeting, 'The Lord Be With You'?

Six times will the Bishop invite us to be with him in prayer as he leads us through the thresholds of our Faith.

Luke 1:28
Ruth 2:4
Galatians 6:18
Philemon 1:3
2 Corinthians 13:14

The Celebrant uses the same words of the Archangel Gabriel when he greeted the Blessed Virgin Mary, "*The Lord is with you*". The first time that we hear this Greeting in the Bible is in the Book of Ruth. This is when Boaz greets a group of harvesters in the wheat fields with the words, "*The Lord be with you. The Lord bless you*". [98]

The Christians of the 2nd Century greeted one another in the same way to remind each other that God was present among them.

Christians at this time understood that they could not praise God correctly during Mass without His Pouring of Grace; therefore their Bishop invited all to let God lead them into Prayer "*The Lord be with you*". [99] In 418 AD Bishop Augustine wrote to his parishioners about this greeting. [100]

"*I greet you, not in my own name only, but in the Name of the Church; and I ask you to pray in unity and sincerity. The Lord be with you.*"

?⃝ **WHY DO WE Respond 'And With Your Spirit'?**

✓ We are praying at this moment for the Celebrant that he may lead us by the Spirit of God.

2 Timothy 4:22
Philemon 1:25

These words, spoken at the opening moments of the Mass, reveal the intimate unity between the Bishop, his Priests and people. The Priest though he may be the main celebrant, is representing his Bishop. It is he who is leading us out of our worldly affairs into the timelessness of the liturgy. And so, we embrace God's Grace by praying for the Bishop. 101

Saint Paul, being aware that we cannot do anything pleasing to our God without His Grace, greeted his communities by saying 102

"The Grace of Our Lord Jesus Christ be with Your Spirit".

St Hippolytus of Rome, c215 AD in the writings of the Apostolic Tradition gave us the first account of instructing the People to welcome God at Mass by praying. 103

"The Lord be with you ... and all shall say ... and with your spirit".

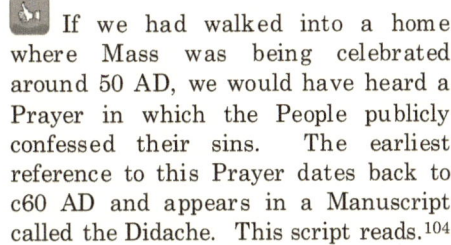 If we had walked into a home where Mass was being celebrated around 50 AD, we would have heard a Prayer in which the People publicly confessed their sins. The earliest reference to this Prayer dates back to c60 AD and appears in a Manuscript called the Didache. This script reads.[104]

"Every Lord's Day do ye gather yourselves together, and Break Bread, and Give Thanksgiving after having Confessed your Transgressions, that your Sacrifice may be Pure."

By c325 AD, only the Bishop prayed in silence, *"I Confess to Almighty God..."* This became known as the *"Confiteor"* or I Confess. They did this in the Sacristy before moving towards the Altar. After 900 AD, they began to repeat this Prayer in front of the Altar at the beginning of the Mass. It was, however, still their private Prayer. [105]

In 1570 AD, Pope Pius V recognized the urgency for everyone to Reconcile with God, and with one another, at the beginning of every Mass. He introduced the Prayer we use today. [106]

"I confess to Almighty God and to You, my Brothers and Sisters, that I have Sinned exceedingly...".

WHY DO WE Pray 'I Confess'?

Each of us takes individual responsibility for our sins as we prepare for Jesus' Sacrifice. [303]

Zechariah 12:10
Revelation 22:14

WHY DO WE Strike Our Chest Three Times?

We purify our hearts as we stand before God the Son, God the Father and God the Holy Spirit.

Luke 23:48
Acts 2:37

St Luke tells us that after Jesus had died on the Cross, the crowd returned to their homes in sorrow striking their breasts. [107] The Church of the 4th Century imitated this by having the Bishops strike their chests three times in the Sacristy before moving towards the Altar. This gesture represented begging the Blessed Trinity for forgiveness. It came to be known as the *"Mea Culpa"*. By c1100 AD, the People had joined their Priest and Bishop in striking their chests three times at the beginning of Mass, as testified by a Monk named Bernold of Constance. [108]

Pope Pius V c1570 allowed all to join in this prayer while striking their chest three times and saying.

"I confess to Almighty God and to You, my Brothers and Sisters that I have sinned, through my fault, through my fault through my most grievous fault'..."

In 1965, the ritual of striking the chest was less common in the English version of the Liturgy, until the year 2011, when the new revision of the Liturgy in English reintroduced it. [109]

WHY DO WE Pray 'Kyrie, Eleison'?

✓ After being purified from our sins, Jesus invites us to enter into His worship, and we praise Him in Greek.

Psalm 51:5
Psalm 118:1

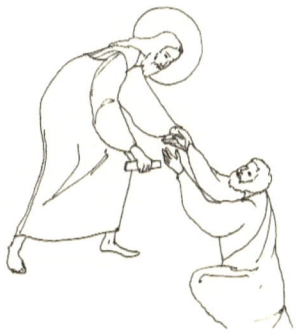

The 2nd Century prayer known as the Kyrie Eleison comes from the Greek words meaning *"Lord, show us your love"*. [110] This was not a petition, but praise directed only to Jesus. The official language for Mass during the 2nd Century was Greek. According to the 4th Century Apostolic Constitutions, Deacons sang a Litany of Short Petitions addressed to Jesus. [111]

"To all these Petitions which the Deacon announces let the People, especially the Children reply Kyrie, Eleison".

In 384 AD, Latin became the official Language of the Mass and these Petitions were progressively shortened until the only Greek response, *"Kyrie Eleison"* remained. After the 12th Century, as the Church felt the need to beg God for mercy for the many sins of it's members, the Kyrie Eleison took the form of a Penitential Prayer meaning, *"Lord, have mercy"*. [112]

When the Ministers chanted the *"Kyrie"* at the beginning of Mass, they were asking the Blessed Trinity to purify them of their sins in order to be worthy of witnessing Jesus' sacrifice, *"Lord have mercy, Christ have mercy, Lord have mercy"*.

WHY DO WE Get Sprinkled With Holy Water?

This is a communal form of purification to prepare us for Jesus' Sacrifice on the Cross.

Numbers 5:17
Psalm 51:7
Leviticus 14:6

The Church of the 2nd Century saw the waters of Baptism as the sign and the bearer of the Divine Life of Grace. [113]

Around 538 AD, Bishop Gregory of Tours described Holy Water as Miraculous. Some people drank it to heal their spiritual and bodily infirmities. Circa 590 AD, Priests, and Deacons began to greet the People as they walked into the Vestibule of the Church by sprinkling them with Holy Water on branches of laurel and olive to purify them from all sin and evil. [114]

By the 6th Century AD, a priest used a metal brush with horse hair attached to the end of the handle and dipped into the Holy Water bucket called Situla or Aspersorium. This brush was known as the Aspergillum from the Latin verb *"Aspergere"* which means to sprinkle. Today the Aspergillum has a sponge instead of hair. During Holy Week, at the Easter Vigil, the Priest blesses the Water to be used for Baptisms and for sprinkling all the baptized during Mass. [115]

? WHY DO WE Proclaim 'Glory To God In The Highest...'?

✓ We imitate the Angels who constantly glorify and honor God, by using their eternal words of praise.

Luke 2:13
Isaiah 25:1
Revelation 4:11

This Hymn reminds the Church that the purpose of life is to Honor God with our lives. We call this Hymn the "*Gloria*" from the Latin word for Glory. The Gloria is the Church's greatest Hymn of Praise. This great Hymn recalls the account of Jesus' birth, and the multitude of Angels who showed up in the Sky singing

"*Glory to God in the Highest, and on Earth, Peace to People of Good Will*". [116]

The 4th Century document "*Apostolic Constitutions*" recorded how a Bishop addressed the People during Mass by saying. [117]

"*Holy Things to the Holy*" after which all responded, "*One Single Holy One, One Single Lord, Jesus Christ, Who is Blessed Forever to the Glory of God the Father. Amen. Glory to God in the Highest*".

By 500 AD, the chanting of the Gloria had become an Official Part of Pope St Symmachus' Midnight Mass at Christmas. [118]

For the following two Centuries, the People only sang the Hymn at the Pope's Masses. However, Priests were gradually allowed to sing the Gloria during Easter Vigil Mass and at their Priestly Anniversaries. By the 11th Century, this concession extended to all Parishes. Everyone chanted the Gloria together with one voice at all Sunday Masses, except during Advent and Lent. Today, the only time that we chant the Gloria during Lent is at the time of the Feast of the Annunciation.

WHY DO WE Hear Scripture Proclaimed From An Ambo?

 Because it suggests a mountaintop or hill from which Christ speaks to us through the Lector.

Matthew 5:1

The word *"Ambo"* comes from the Greek word meaning Elevation. When the Persecution of Christians in Rome had ended after Christianity was accepted, the Liturgy steadily became more formalized. By the 4th Century, the Church had defined which Books should form the Bible. Sacred Scripture was treated with such Dignity and Adoration that it required its own place on the Altar. As early as 320 AD, ambos, or pulpits, were found in the main Nave of the Basilica. [119]

For more than one thousand years, there were no pews in Churches, and Christians stood while listening to the Proclamation of the Scriptures. In those days, the Ambo literally served as a Mountaintop for God's Word. [120] It was often shaped like a Chalice, with steps leading up to the top where the Minister stood. Over his head, there was a small canopy that served as a sounding board to reflect his voice. [121]

These days we sit during Readings, except for the Proclamation of the Holy Gospel.

 **WHY DO WE Sit In Mass?**

✓ It is a suitable posture for reflecting on the Scripture for the day, the homily, at the Offertory and after Communion

Luke 10:39
Matthew 5:1
Ephesians 2:6

During the first two centuries, Mass was said in private homes; seats were limited. Christians started the tradition of giving up their seat for the elderly, poor and infirm. [122]

After the Emperor Constantine had accepted Christianity in 313 AD, he donated 25 public buildings to the Church. These structures did not have pews or kneelers and so only the ill and elderly sat on benches along the walls. The Bishop sat in his Teaching Chair to preach called in Greek "*Cathedra*". During the 9th Century, Monks were the first ones to sit at Mass. They sat in wooden seats between the Altar and the People known as the Choir. German monks began to call this seat a "*Bangk*" or Bench. [123]

In the 12th Century, wealthy German merchants brought their own custom-made "*Bangks*" to Mass, which they took home with them every Sunday. During the week, they conducted the business of lending money to customers while sitting on their church bench. Their business activities came to be known as Banks. [272]

By 1300 AD, some churches were furnished with simple benches. People, however, had begun to bring their own low profile stools and mats. In 1530, all churches officially began to provide benches with backs they called in French "*Puye*" or Pew. This was a reflection of the Church placing greater emphasis on listening to the Word of God in Scripture and in the Homily. [124]

WHY DO WE Proclaim Scripture From The Lectionary Book?

A Lector lends voice to the Word of God for all the Scripture Readings except for the Gospel.

Romans 10:17
Luke 24:44
John 20:24
1 Samuel 3:10

Many Christians in the 2nd Century had to frequent Synagogues in order to hear the Written Word of God. A Church was privileged in those early days to have a copy of a Gospel or a Letter from St. Paul. The Bible as we know it was incomplete in those early days. By 90 AD, at the Jewish Council of Jamnia Jewish Rabbis agreed upon the books that would form the Hebrew Bible. 292 By 100 AD, the New Testament writings were completed, but the final set of Old Testament Books was not agreed until 250 AD. The "Muratorian Cannon" is the oldest manuscript preserved suggesting the books to form the Bible and which were still doubtful like the Apocalypse of Peter, Hebrews and Revelation. 125

By 260 AD, The Legends of Martyrs and of Saints, the Gospels and the other Prayers that Deacons chanted in Mass were collected in a book known as the Lectionary Book. 126

In 393 AD, the Synod of Hippo in Algeria agreed upon the final content of the entire Bible. After that, St Jerome translated the Bible into Latin in the year 405 AD so that all the People could easily read and understand it. 127

By the 6th Century, Christians had their first fully structured Lectionary, with readings from all 73 Bible Books for every day of the week. The Council of Trent finally approved all 73 Books of the Bible in 1563. The Protestant Bible contains only 66 of these books.

WHY DO WE HEAR Different Readings Every Day At Mass?

They follow a Three-Year Cycle, set out in such a way that that anybody attending Daily Mass would have heard the entire Bible in three years.

Ezekiel 37:4
John 21:2

Christians adopted the Three-Year Cycle from the Jews of the 2nd Century. Every Sabbath Day, Jews in every Synagogue read the Torah. It was read in Sections to ensure that the entire Law would be heard in three years. The first converts to Christianity were of Jewish origin. In order to listen and pray with the Old Testament Scriptures, they continued to attend the Synagogues until they were no longer welcomed in the year 100 AD. After this event, they began to gather at homes for the Morning Scripture Proclamation which was opened for both baptized and the non-baptized. [128]

By 400 AD, the Morning Scripture Proclamation became part of the Mass as we have it today. Pope Gregory I, in 590 AD, adopted three reading Cycles for the Readings of the Gospels. These Readings were arranged as Cycle A, relying on the Gospel of St Matthew, Cycle B, for the Gospel of St Mark, and Cycle C, for the Gospel of St Luke. St John's Gospel was read throughout the three Cycles. Every Sunday, people listened to One Epistle, the Responsorial Psalm and the Gospel. In 1965, The Church provided the Faithful with the Second Epistle after the Responsorial Psalm. Because,

"*Ignorance of the Scriptures is Ignorance of Christ.*" [129]

WHY DO WE Recite Or Sing A Psalm?

✅ The Psalms reflect every expression of human emotion. They help us rejoice, cry, and express our thanksgiving to God through song or recitation.

Psalm 47:7

🔊 The Psalter is a Compendium of 150 Hebrew Psalms. It is also a Book in which the Word of God becomes the People's Prayer. During Jesus' time, the singing of the Psalms in synagogues, at home and at festivals was a regular event; compared to past generations where Hebrews were not allowed to sing Psalms outside of the Temple Ceremonies at all. [130]

For 2nd Century Christians, the Psalms became a Prayerful Response to their sorrows and joys. Officially, Pope Celestine I in 422 AD introduced the Responsorial Psalm into the Liturgy. [131] Since then, the Community has gathered at Mass to hear the Cantor proclaim the Verses of a Psalm as the People respond with a Refrain. [132]

The Church ensures that only Hymns that paraphrase the Psalms are used at this time. Indeed, as Saint Augustine wrote, "*Qui cantat bis orat*", or "*Who sings prays twice*".[133] Then he added. [134]

"*Dear Friends, sing the Psalms with human reason, not like parrots. They are often taught to say what they do not understand, but we can know what we are saying by God's Grace. So, we who are taught to sing about God's Works should be eager to do so, singing together with one voice*".

WHAT IS THE Difference Between Psalms, Hymns, And Chants?

A Psalm is a Poem from the Book of Psalms. A Chant is a short musical passage in which Psalms are used. A hymn is a song of praise to God.

Psalm 149:3
Psalm 33:2
Revelation 14:2

The Greek word for Poem is "*Psalmos*". The Collection of 150 Psalms in the Bible is known as the Book of Psalms. These poems, from around 970 BC, are attributed to King David. They were to be sung to the accompaniment of a harp. [135]

The Greek word for a Song of Joy is "*Hymnos*". Hymns for ancient Greeks were story-songs about their gods protecting their favored people. Hymns for Christians in late 300 AD were Songs of Praise to God for giving us Jesus as our Savior, the Blessed Virgin Mary as our Mother, and the Saints as examples for us to follow.

In 590 AD, Pope Gregory I instructed Churches to select groups of trained voices called Choirs to represent the Voices of the People during Mass. The Members of these Choirs were taught to understand the Pope's Gregorian Chant, which remains the oldest notated form of music known to us. [136]

In the 9th Century, Choirs stood between the Sanctuary and the Congregation. By the 16th Century, they sat in balconies at the back of Churches instead. Their singing of Psalms and Hymns came to be known as Chanting.

WHY DO WE Recite The Alleluia?

☑ It's like giving God a Standing Ovation. It's the Assembly's Homage to God for Allowing us to experience Christ's Words in the Gospel.

Revelation 19
Psalm 150:6

The two Hebrew words forming the Alleluia are "*Hall el*" meaning *Praise,* and "*Yah,*" the Hebrew name for *God.* They had been sung every Sabbath Day in every Synagogue since before the 1st Century AD, when Torah Scrolls were brought from the Ark in the Temple of Jerusalem and placed upon the Reading Stand. [137]

In the Book of Revelation, the writer sees Blessed Men and Women in Heaven singing "*Hall el-Yah*" constantly before God.   2nd Century Christians chanted the Alleluia during Mass after Praying Amen. St Augustine reminded his Parishioners in 430 AD,

"*We are an Easter People, and Alleluia is our Song*". [138]

The Communities of the 5th Century knew that Christianity was not just for Sundays but for every hour of every day as well. Therefore, they had a saying "*A Christian is an Alleluia from Head to Toe*". [139]

By 540 AD, the Proclamation of the Alleluia before the Gospel was customary in most Churches as is testified by St Benedict in his Rule for Monasteries. [140 & 141]

"*Alleluia often serves as an Acclamation during the Procession for the Gospel*".

Today, the only time that we do not sing the Alleluia is during Lent as we await Jesus' Resurrection.

WHY DO WE Stand For The Gospel Acclamation?

The Bible says that Angels stand firm before God To Praise and Listen to Him. We imitate the Angels.

Nehemiah 9:5
Matthew 4:23
Zechariah 6:5
Ezra 9:15
Jeremiah 15:1

We stand firm for the Gospel Reading just as the Christians of the 4th Century did. Gospel comes from the Greek word "*Evangelium*", meaning Glad Tidings. [142]

In 382 AD, Pope Damasus I, at the Council of Rome, approved the Four Gospels to be proclaimed during Mass: Mark, Matthew, Luke, and John. These Gospels together record the Life and Teachings of Christ. Before that date, there were more than 20 gospel writings available to the Christian community, many of these written by disciples using erroneous teachings. Some were attributed to Peter or Thomas the Apostle. The Church needed to clarify which Books were authentic. [143]

Before printing presses arrived, Monks dedicated their lives to transcribing the Gospels by hand, with each one taking them many years to complete.

The Holy Book used in Mass containing these Four Gospels was called the Book of Gospels. Some Books of Gospels were bound in gold and precious stones and placed on the Altar after Mass for adoration and worship. Today, the Church reveres the Gospels greatly. Only an ordained Minister may proclaim one in Mass and people have to stand up in adoration. [144]

WHY DO WE Sign Ourselves With Three Crosses Before The Gospel?

The Gospel is Jesus Himself. We welcome Him and we impress His Word with our thumbs into our minds, lips, and hearts.

Hebrews 4:12
Ezekiel 3:1
Deuteronomy 8:3

The Cross is by far the most powerful Symbol for all Christians. In 387 AD, St Augustine explained that by making three small Signs of the Cross with our thumbs before the Gospel Proclamation, we are driving away Satan who seeks to destroy us, and welcoming the One who gives us Life.[145]

When a Minister says, "*A Reading from the Holy Gospel according to...*" he simultaneously traces a small Cross on the Gospel Page with his thumb. Then, with the same thumb, he makes three more small Crosses, one on his forehead, one on his lips and one on his chest. The Congregation does the same. The Church has continued with this 4th Century ritual so that the Living Word of God about to be proclaimed is impressed into our thinking, into our speaking and into our hearts. [146] The Bible commands us in Ezekiel, to Eat the Sacred Scroll of God's Word, so it becomes our nourishment for Life. [147]

WHY DO WE Hear A Homily?

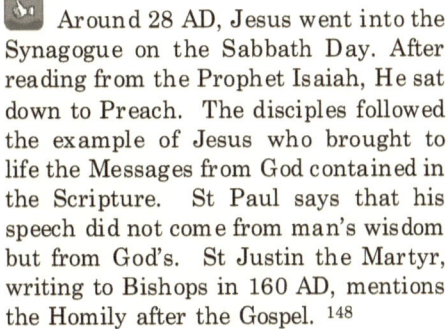 This is the moment to be inspired with deep Faith, when we fully comprehend all that God has done for us.

Luke 24:45
Isaiah 61:1
Hebrews 4:12
1 Corinthians 2:4

Around 28 AD, Jesus went into the Synagogue on the Sabbath Day. After reading from the Prophet Isaiah, He sat down to Preach. The disciples followed the example of Jesus who brought to life the Messages from God contained in the Scripture. St Paul says that his speech did not come from man's wisdom but from God's. St Justin the Martyr, writing to Bishops in 160 AD, mentions the Homily after the Gospel. [148]

"Then, when the Reader has finished, the Presider verbally gives a warning, and appeals for the imitation of these good examples".

In 270 AD, Bishop Samosata of Antioch asked people not to clap or cheer after a good sermon. During the 4th Century, the Church began to distinguish between two different kinds of Preaching: the Instruction, or in Greek "*Homilia*" the Homily, and the Conversation or in Latin, "*Sermo*" or the Sermon. The "*Homilia*" was a more formal, doctrinal and scriptural based form of preaching founded on the Readings of the Day. The "*Sermo*" by contrast, was more a spiritual, catechetical, interactive conversation that followed a different theme from that which was proclaimed in that Sunday's Scriptures. [273]

In 1965, Vatican II selected the Homily as the best form of preaching. Today the Church requires that a Homily be preached on Sundays, and on other Holy Days of Obligation. A Bishop, Priest, or Deacon is the only one allowed to preach a Homily. [149]

WHY DO WE Recite The Creed By Saying 'I Believe'?

 This is the Profession of our Faith. It defines who we are as Catholics and Who God Is for us. We recite what we know to be true.

Matthew 28:19
Mark 16:19
Luke 1:4
1 Corinthians 15:3

The word Creed comes from the Latin "*Credo*" meaning, I believe. We say "*I Believe*" instead of "*We Believe*" because even though we participate in the Sacraments as a Community each and every one of us still holds Personal Responsibility for our Faith in Jesus. [150]

The Christians of the 2nd Century AD proclaimed a basic Creed. According to St Hippolytus in 217 AD, as new Believers entered the Pool of Baptism, the Minister asked them. [151]

"*Do you believe in God the Father Almighty, Maker of Heaven and Earth? ... Do you believe in Jesus Christ, His only Son and Lord ... Do you believe in the Holy Spirit ...?*". To which, each Candidate responded "*I Believe*" and then was immersed in the Waters.

At the Council of Nicea in 325 AD, the full Statement of our Belief was confirmed. This came to be known as the Nicene Creed. [152] At first the Creed was recited only during Baptisms. We know it was never recited during Sunday Mass until the 11th Century, when it became officially part of the Liturgy. [153] In 1965, the Creed was translated from Latin into English as "*We Believe*," and in 2011, the Church brought back its original meaning "*I Believe*". [154]

? WHY DO WE Recite The Prayers Of The Faithful?

✓ This represents the way the universal Church prays for the global needs of all peoples.

1 Thessalonians 5:17

The Prayers of the Faithful are in the form of a Litany. First comes the petition prayer, followed by an invitation, "*We Pray to the Lord*". The response that follows from the entire congregation is normally, "*Lord Hear Our Prayer*".

Praying for the intentions of others is a Jewish tradition that began in synagogues during the 1st Century AD. Jews living at the time of Christ prayed a total of 18 blessings every morning for those in need. When 2nd Century Christians gathered in their homes for Mass they continued with this custom. [155]

Those who were not yet baptized left Mass after the proclamation of the Gospel. Only the baptized faithful remained for the Eucharistic Sacrifice. This moment began with the petition Litanies for the needs of all the Church. Christians called these petitions "*Prayers of the Faithful.*" As early as the 5th Century, the Apostolic Constitutions described how the baptized faithful responded to various Mass Petitions by saying "*Lord, Show us Your Love*", in Greek, "*Kyrie Eleison*". [156]

In 1965, the Church confirmed that these Prayers should be for the needs of the Church, for public authorities, for the salvation of the whole world, for those burdened by all kinds of difficulty, and for the local community. [157]

WHY DO WE Give Money During Sunday Collection?

All our gifts are from God and thus they belong to Him. We administer them and give a portion back in the Sunday Collection.

Galatians 2:10
Romans 15:25
Deuteronomy 14:22
1 Corinthians 16:1
2 Corinthians 8:9
Luke 21:1

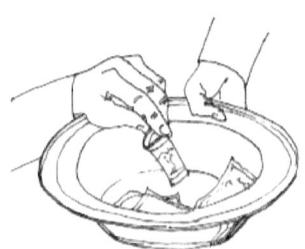

The Sunday Collection is a part of Mass that has remained unchanged since 150 AD. From the start, the Christian community gave back to God part of the fruit of their labor during the Sunday Collection. This reminded them to trust in God, for He provided for their needs.[158] St Paul writing to the Parishes in Galatia told them to bring something for the Offertory.

"On the first day of the week each of you should set aside and save whatever one can afford".

St. Justin the Martyr was the first Bishop to describe the Sunday Collection of 165 AD. [159]

"The wealthy among us help the needy, and we always lend one another assistance: those who desire to make gifts, each just as he wishes. These gifts are collected and handed over to the Presider. It is he who assists the Orphans and Widows, Those who are in Want through Sickness or for some other reason, Prisoners, and Strangers passing through briefly".

The Bible in the Book of Deuteronomy reminds us that one tenth of our income belongs to God. This is known as Tithing.

"Each year you shall tithe all the produce that grows in the field you have sown".

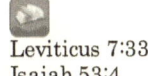 WHY DO WE Bring Gifts Up To The Minister During The Offertory?

The family processing represents each of us coming towards the Altar to offer ourselves with Jesus for the Sacrifice.

Leviticus 7:33
Isaiah 53:4

The Offertory has been known as the moment of Divine Exchange. [160] Not only did the Christians of the 2nd Century give ten percent of their money back to God, they also handed back themselves represented in the gifts of Bread and Wine. [161] In return, God exchanged Himself by giving them His Body and Blood. [162]

After 313 AD, Families processed during the Offertory to offer their personal gifts. The poorer Christians, who could not provide financial help, presented any other gifts they could give, such as cheese, oil, candles, wheat, grapes, and other foods. These helped sustain the Clergy and the Poor. They did not give their gifts directly to the Bishop though but to their Deacons, who placed them on tables to the left and right side of the Altar. [163] This ritual was interrupted around the year 800 AD. [281] At this time, the Credence Table was created. A small side table in the Sanctuary containing on it the Chalice, Paten with the Host, the Cruets with wine and water and the Bowl, Ewer and Towel for the Lavabo and Ablution after Communion. Credence in Latin means "*Believing*".

In 1965, Vatican II reinstituted the ritual and today one family takes the Gifts of Bread and Wine to the Altar, and they represent all of us present at Holy Mass. [164]

 **WHY DO WE Worship In Church Facing East?**

Because we are facing Christ Himself who is the rising sun, the new dawn, the light of the world.

Daniel 6:10
Matthew 24:27

Since the 2nd Century, all Christians began to say their Morning Prayers facing eastwards towards the rising sun. Jesus Christ as the new Light of the World was their premier symbol. When these Christians, at Baptism, renounced Satan, they faced west, and when they accepted Jesus, they turned to face east. Also, they knew that Jesus would return again from the east. As soon as these Christians arrived in Rome they turned their Altars east, not only towards the rising sun but also towards Jerusalem where their Lord Jesus was crucified.[165]

"Pray facing east, for it is written: Give thanks to God who rides on the eastern side of the highest heavens". The Didascalia, c250 AD

In 313 AD, When Emperor Constantine donated public buildings to the Church, their facades faced east. The rising sun fell on the Minister as he stood behind the Altar facing east and his people, this came to be known in Latin as *"Ad Orientem"*. By the 8th Century, all new churches in Rome were built so the people and the Priest also faced East *"Ad Orientem"*, though now it seemed as though the priest had his back to his congregation. [166] After Vatican II, most churches changed the position of their Altars, so both people and the Priest faced the Altar, the Cross of Christ. Today, the Church sees both orientations as valid and encourages *"Ad Orientem"* when possible. [167]

WHY DO WE See A Corporal On Top Of The Altar?

✓ This linen helps the Priest define which Bread and what Chalices with Wine will become the Bread and Blood of Christ.

1 Samuel 28:2

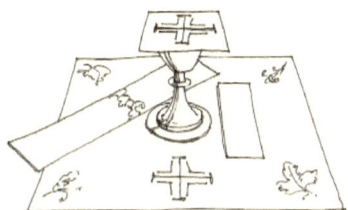

A Corporal is a square white linen cloth placed across the Altar during the Offertory. Corporal comes from the Latin word *"Corpus"* meaning *body*. During Jesus' time Roman army corporals formed their commander's personal bodyguard, ready to defend their senior officer with their lives. In a similar way, the Corporal is there to guard which Bread and Wine will become Body and Blood of Christ. [168]

Around 335 AD, Pope Sylvester I prescribed the Corporal for the first time. He ordained that it lay across the Altar Cloth to receive the Particles that fell from the Breaking of the Bread. Pope Benedict XIV, in 1740 AD, said that any Bread or Wine placed outside the limits of a Corporal does not become the Body and Blood of Christ unless the Priest had the intention but did not realize they rested outside the Corporal. Every Corporal is blessed with a Special Prayer before it may be used. It must be disposed by burning if it becomes torn since it was used for the Sacred Sacrifice of Jesus. [169]

WHY DO WE See A Paten On The Altar?

By placing Bread in the Paten, the Priest offers it to God to be transformed into the Body of Christ. [170]

John 6:58

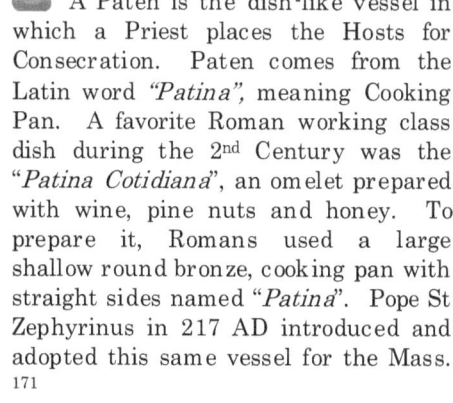 A Paten is the dish-like vessel in which a Priest places the Hosts for Consecration. Paten comes from the Latin word *"Patina"*, meaning Cooking Pan. A favorite Roman working class dish during the 2nd Century was the *"Patina Cotidiana"*, an omelet prepared with wine, pine nuts and honey. To prepare it, Romans used a large shallow round bronze, cooking pan with straight sides named *"Patina"*. Pope St Zephyrinus in 217 AD introduced and adopted this same vessel for the Mass. [171]

By the 4th Century, all Patens were made of silver. The Deacon passed it among the Congregation, and each Family placed their Bread Offering in it for the Sacrifice. After the Prayer for Consecration, the Presider would break the Eucharistic Bread into small pieces, and place these Fragments inside the Paten for Distribution as Communion. [298] During the 9th Century, the People no longer brought Bread for the Eucharistic Meal. Instead, Monasteries began to bake unleavened bread and thus the Paten was reduced in size. [172]

WHY DO WE See A Host On the Altar?

This white wafer is being offered to God, blessed and soon will become the Body of Christ.

Isaiah 53:3
Exodus 29:23
1 Corinthians 11:23

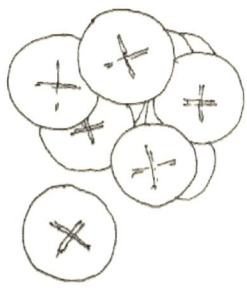

Host comes from the Latin word, "*Hostia*" meaning Victim or Enemy. Around 520 BC, the Romans began to sacrifice their enemies of war or hostages in order to gain good fortune from their gods. Christians of the 2nd Century called Jesus in the Eucharistic Bread the Passover Victim, because He was Sacrificed as the enemy on the Cross. [173]

The custom of baking Hosts Bread without yeast goes back to Jesus' Passover Meal. This signified the hasty departure of the Jewish people from slavery in Egypt. Some 2nd Century Christians continued with this custom. Others made sure that their Host Bread had yeast as they wanted to distance themselves from Jewish traditions. [174] They added two "*X*" symbols on their breads to signify the Cross, and the name of Christ.

In 798 AD, Charlemagne's advisor Alcuin prescribed Unleavened Bread for Churches in Rome. At this time, there was only one Large Host Consecrated for all to receive Communion. In 1439 AD, at the Council of Florence, the Church prescribed for all Parishes that all Hosts should be made without yeast. In 1576 AD, the Council of Milan set guidelines for making Hosts in Monasteries. In the 17th Century, iron molds were used to make small round Hosts very much like the ones we have today. [175]

WHY DO WE See A Chalice On The Altar?

This Cup is placed on top of the Corporal and holds the Wine to become the Blood of Christ.

1 Corinthian 10:14
1 Timothy 1:23

The word Chalice comes from the Latin word, '*Calix*' meaning Cup. The use of a Chalice at Mass comes from the Last Supper, c29 AD. When Jesus celebrated His Last Passover Meal, every Apostle at the Table had three small cups of wine while a large Chalice filled with Wine called the Cup of Blessing stood at the center of the table. This Main Cup is the One to which Jesus added his own Blessing "*This is My Blood, which will be Given Up for You*". What He handed to His Apostles was therefore, no longer a ritual cup of wine. It was a Holy Chalice with His own Blood inside.

In 397 AD, Saint John Chrysostom described this moment. [176]

"*The Table was not of Silver, the Chalice in which Christ Gave His Blood to His Disciples to Drink was not of Gold. Yet Everything was Precious and Truly Fit to inspire Awe*".

The oldest Chalice still in existence dates from 518 AD and is currently in the Imperial Library in Paris, France. The Church has always understood that when it comes to Mass there is no Vow of Poverty, just Quiet Dignity at the Summit of Church Life.

The Chalice for the Mass may be a simple or an ornate vessel. It must, however, be made of precious material such as gold, or at least be gold plated inside the Cup. [177]

WHY DO WE See A Pall And Purificator On Top Of The Chalice?

The Purificator is a linen cloth used for cleaning and drying the Chalice. The Pall's function is to cover it from dust.

Luke 22:10

The word Pall comes from the Latin word, "*Palla*," meaning Cover. This stiff square linen piece covers the Chalice during the Sacrifice. [178] In 1st Century Rome, women wore a shawl over their dresses, known as "*Palla*". The Church in the 3rd Century adopted this name for the linen covering the entire Altar, later known as Altar Cloth. The Pall also covered the Coffins of Popes or Bishops during funerals. By the 4th Century, the Bishops needed a new form of linen to cover the Chalice keeping dust and insects from falling into it. To solve this, they came up with a new, hard, stiff linen cover, which they also called the Pall. [179]

The 4th Century Roman Church came up with a white rectangular linen cloth needed for cleaning out and drying the Chalice, Paten, Ciborium and other vessels after Communion, or while Distributing the Blood of Christ. They called it the Purificator. Today, when we receive Communion and drink of the Blood of Christ, the Minister wipes the rim of the Chalice with the Purificator - no other linen is allowed. The Purificator does not require a particular Prayer of Blessing in order to be used. [177]

WHY DO WE See A Chalice Veil On The Altar?

It protects the Chalice from dust when not in use. It also reminds us of the Jewish Tabernacle that was covered from the elements with fine linens.

Exodus 26:1

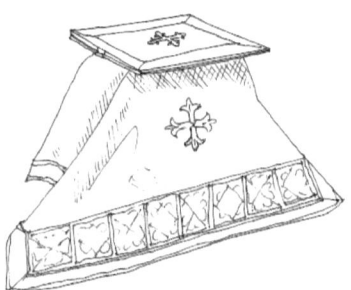

Since the year 800 AD, people had stopped receiving the Blood of Christ at Communion. Thus, there was need only for one Chalice. At that time, families no longer brought the Wine to the Priest during the Offering of the Gifts as was previously customary. A veil was needed to cover the Chalice until brought to the Altar by the Priest. This was the origin of the Chalice Veil.

On the Altar, a colored Veil covered the Chalice, Pall, Paten and Purificator according to the liturgical colors of the year. The Corporal rested inside an envelope-like container covered in fine linen, called the Burse. The Burse was placed on top of the Chalice Veil. The use of the Chalice Veil became official in 1502 AD by Pope Alexander IV. Today, the Church no longer prescribes the use of a Veil. It does, however, praise its value, and directs that the color of the veil, where used, may be either white, or follow the liturgical color of the season. [180]

WHY DO WE See A Ciborium On The Altar?

 The Ciborium is a precious vessel shaped like a lotus that holds already Consecrated Hosts. [181]

Exodus 27:19
John 6:58

Ciborium comes from the Latin word "*Cibus*", meaning Food. This dish has its origins in 7th Century BC Egypt. 3rd Century Christians reserved the Body of Christ within a box called the Pyx for those ill and dying. By the 7th Century, a much larger Pyx was needed to reserve larger amounts of the Eucharist in Church. They adopted the idea from the Egyptian Ciborium, a drinking cup in the form of a lotus, symbol of eternal life and added a cover topped by a small Cross. This vessel was kept hidden inside the Tabernacle in the Sacristy. [182]

In the 13th Century, Churches began to build large Canopies shaped like Cups above their Altars. These were also called Ciboria or Baldachins. Their purpose was to protect the Altar from debris or dust falling from the ceiling. A Ciborium built over an Altar also facilitated the suspension of the Tabernacle over it.

WHY DO Priests Mix Water And Wine In The Chalice?

The Church views this ritual as the Symbolic Union of Christ's Divinity mixed with our Humanity.

John 19:34
Isaiah 1:22
Jeremiah 25:30
Jeremiah 38:33
Zechariah 10:7
Song of Songs 5:1
1 Timothy 5:23

The custom of mixing a little Water to the Wine began in Jewish homes centuries before Christianity evolved. This was a practical way of diminishing its alcoholic content since the Wines in Lebanon and Palestine were strong. Good Wine was a sign for Israelites that God was happy with them. [183] The Book of the Prophet Zechariah describes God's blessing as "*Their hearts will be cheered as though by wine.*"

2nd century Christians saw wine as a sign of healing, love and fraternal friendship. Water was a sign of the humanity redeemed through Baptismal Water. [90] For these Christians, the addition of Water to the Wine at Mass also had a deeper spiritual meaning. Sin weakens humanity and the Wine was watered down to remind them of this fact. In the 6th Century, the mixing became a symbol of the two natures of Christ, the Divine and the Human. The Water suggested that which flowed from the side of Christ Crucified when pierced by a lance. [184]

When a Minister mixes Water in the Chalice, he prays, [185]

"*By the mystery of this water and this wine may we come to share in the Divinity of Christ, who Humbled Himself to share in Our Humanity.*"

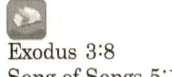 **WHY DID Bishops Used To Add Honey And Milk to The Wine At Mass?**

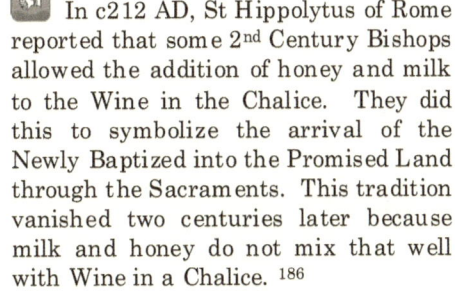 This was a symbol of the Promised Land, which flowed in milk and honey.

Exodus 3:8
Song of Songs 5:1

In c212 AD, St Hippolytus of Rome reported that some 2nd Century Bishops allowed the addition of honey and milk to the Wine in the Chalice. They did this to symbolize the arrival of the Newly Baptized into the Promised Land through the Sacraments. This tradition vanished two centuries later because milk and honey do not mix that well with Wine in a Chalice. [186]

"The Deacons immediately bring the offering to the bishop, who by giving thanks, shall make the cup of wine mixed with water into the likeness of his blood, which is shed for all who believe in him. Milk and honey shall be mixed together in fulfillment of the promise given to the patriarchs, of a land flowing with milk and honey"

WHY DO WE Hear The Prayer Over Gifts During The Offertory?

✓ He offers the Bread and Wine to God, the Holy Spirit and asks to bless them.

Genesis 33:10
Daniel 3:39
Deuteronomy 8:10

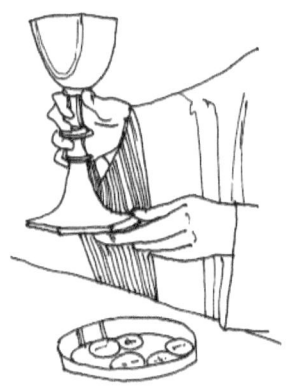

We watch a Priest bow profoundly as he offers the Gifts to God, asking the Holy Spirit to bless them. [187]

"With Humble Spirit and Contrite Heart may We be Accepted by You, O Lord, and may Our Sacrifice in Your Sight This Day be Pleasing to You, Lord God".

During Jesus' time, on the eve of every Sabbath all Jewish families celebrated a Fellowship Meal, called the '*Chaburah*'. This Meal began with a Blessing over the cup of wine and dish of bread, when they prayed,

"Blessed are you, O Lord our God, King of the Universe, Creator of the Fruit of the Vine...".

The family present at the table would respond *"Blessed be God Forever".* Jesus did the same at the Seder Meal of 29 AD before transforming the bread into his Flesh. Since then, Christians throughout the centuries have *Said Grace* before meals.

"Bless us oh Lord, and these thy gifts which we are about to receive from thy bounty, through Christ, our Lord."

Jewish converts adopted the same Jewish prayer for the Blessing of the Cup of Wine and of Bread at the Offertory in Mass. This Prayer was recited aloud during the 2nd Century Liturgy. However in the 5th Century, the Bishops of Byzantium in Turkey decided to pray it in silence instead. They wanted to add more reverence to the Mass. In 1965, this prayer was returned to its original form. [188]

WHY DO WE See Priests Use Incense?

By Incensing the Altar, the Book of Gospels, and the Gifts of Bread and Wine, the Priest Honors God who is All-Holy.

Psalm 14:1
Psalm 141:2
1 Peter 2:9
Exodus 19:6
Isaiah 43:20
Malachi 3:17
Revelation 8:3

Incense comes from a Latin word "*Incendere*" meaning Burning. During Jesus' time, it was customary for a Jewish Priest to use Incense in the Temple to Bless the Gifts for the Sacrifice. The rising smoke and the aromas symbolized God accepting His People's Petitions and Prayers. According to an Apocryphal Gospel, Jesus used incense during His Last Supper meal. [264] The Romans used incense to honor their royal people, their senators and their emperors. [189]

The Thurifer is the Minister in charge of Incense. During Mass, he takes a spoon of Incense from a metal container called the Incense Boat, and pours this inside a Thurible Bowl, a metal censer suspended from chains, containing hot coals to heat it. After that, the Priest makes a Sign of the Cross over it for the Blessing. [190]

Incense first appeared at Mass in 320 AD after Emperor Constantine granted Christians the right of use. Only that which is Royal, or Holy, is Worthy to be Incensed. The Church Incenses Ministers and every Person in the Congregation, in order to remind them of their Baptismal Royalty.

WHY DO WE See Priests Wash Their Hands During the Offertory?

 This Ritual is a symbol of Cleansing of Sin, in order to Represent Christ Worthily before the Altar. 303

Psalm 25:6
Psalm 26:6
Psalm 51:2
John 13:8
Exodus 30:17

The 1st Century Mediterranean belief stated that any person's soul was visible through three windows. That person's face, mouth and hands. It followed that cleansing any of these three attributes would purify the soul.191 During this Century, a Jewish Priest would wash his feet and hands before he sacrificed any animal at an Altar. Water was a symbol for purity.

The ritual for the Passover Meal required those at the table to wash their hands twice before touching the Bread. At Jesus' Mass c29 AD, he washed the feet of his disciples instead.192

This ritual soon became part of Mass in the 2nd Century, when an Altar Server held a bowl, and a towel as he poured water from an Ewer onto the Bishop's hands. After 325 AD, Basilicas filled with Converts who brought all kinds of gifts, for the Offertory including produce. Bishops washed their hands after receiving these gifts.193 With time, this ritual became known as "*Lavame Domine*" or Wash me Lord.

As the Priest washes his hands he prays the words from the Bible softly "*Lord, wash away my iniquity and cleanse me from my sin*".

After Mass, this water may only go down a particular sink located in the Sacristy, called the Lavabo, which drains directly to the ground. Alternatively, it may moisten plants to signify impure water that must return to earth. 194

WHY DO WE Hear 'Pray, Brethren that My Sacrifice And Yours May Be Acceptable To God'?

✓ The Priest, feeling unworthy to be at the Sacrifice, turns to us and invites us to stand up and pray with him. [195]

Genesis 4:5
Malachi 1:10

During the Liturgy of the 2nd Century, a Bishop said a Blessing over Bread and Wine placed on the Altar Table. There was, however, no invitation from the Minister for People to offer a Personal Offering United to his. [196]

No Invitation like this existed until 700 AD, when the Churches of France and Germany allowed People to offer a Prayer of Sacrifice in unison with their Priest. The Priest said,

"*Pray Brethren that Our Sacrifice may be Acceptable to God our Father*".

However, the Response from the Faithful remained just a Reverent Silence. [197]

By the 11th Century, all the Churches had adopted the Response from the People similar to what we say today.

"*May the Lord accept the Sacrifice from thy hands, to the Praise and Glory of His Name, for our benefit and for that of all His Church*".

This prayer came to be known as the '*Orate Fratres*', in Latin meaning, Let us Pray, Brethren. [198]

WHY DO WE Respond 'It Is Right And Just' After The 'Lift Up Your Hearts'?

 Our only Focus and Disposition at this moment is of humble Thanksgiving to God for finding us worthy to stand before His Altar.

Psalm 141: 2
Revelation 4:5
Leviticus 24:3
Hebrews 12:18
1 Timothy 3:16
Lamentations 3:41

The Book of Revelation tells us that the Saints in Heaven stretch their hearts on high in Worship before God. "*Hearts on High*", or '*Sursum Corda*', is what the Priest asks us to possess as our Right and Just disposition before we partake of the Sacrifice. [199]

This is a truly Ancient Prayer. The first record we have of it comes from Bishop St Hippolytus c217 AD. [200]

"Let him say the Words of Thanksgiving ... Let us Lift up our Hearts ... They are Turned to the Lord ... Let us give Thanks to the Lord our God. It is Right and Just".

In a Homily from 380 AD, Bishop Cyril of Jerusalem said, [201]

"It is as if the Priest is instructing us to dismiss all physical cares and domestic anxieties, and to Have our Hearts in Heaven with the Benevolent God. Then you answer 'We Lift Them Up to The Lord". In other words you give assent to what the Priest has said. Certainly we ought to give Thanks to God for having invited us, unworthy as we are, to such a great gift. We ought to give thanks to God for reconciling us to Himself when we were His enemies. We ought to give Thanks to God for having made us His Adopted Children by the Spirit. Then you say – It is Right and Just'.

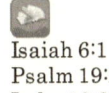 **WHY DO WE Say 'Holy, Holy, Holy Lord God of Hosts.'?**

✓ We are about to start the Eucharistic Prayer, and we do so by giving Glory and Honor to God, the Trinity, by calling Him The All-Holy.

Isaiah 6:1
Psalm 19:2
Luke 19:38

The 1ˢᵗ Century Jewish Sabbath Prayers in Synagogue began with the Invocation "*Kadosh, Kadosh, Kadosh*". This was from words by the Prophet Isaiah describing how the Angels praised God while covering their faces with their wings in outmost awe, Holy, Holy, Holy. The Hebrew word "*Kadosh*" means set apart from imperfection. Jewish people may not pronounce God's Name out of respect. 202

Hebrew has no way to express the degrees of an adjective other than to repeat the same word twice, and anything referring to God three times, like saying, "*Holy, Holier, Holiest*". Therefore, when the Christian Community in the 2ⁿᵈ Century sang, "*Holy, Holy, Holy Lord God of Hosts, Heaven and Earth are Full of Your Glory...*" it was their most honorable way of praising God. 203

Around 230 AD, the Church in Alexandria, Egypt began to chant this Prayer at Mass. They concluded the chant with words spoken by crowds on Palm Sunday as Jesus entered Jerusalem "*Hosanna in the Highest*". The Hebrew word "*Hosanna*" is a cry for help "... we *ask you, save us*". By adding, "*...in the highest*" they placed added urgency implying "*really* ... we mean it ... please do it now". Since then, throughout the world, Christians adore the Blessed Trinity with this prayer. 204

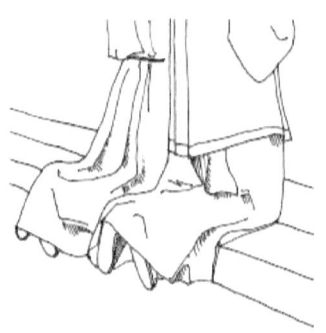 **WHY DO WE Kneel Or Stand During the Eucharistic Prayer?**

When we stand we show our readiness to God, when we kneel we show our humility as He Offers Himself for our sins at the Altar.

Philippians 2:10
Romans 5:2
1 Peter 5:12
Ezra 9:15
Psalm 5:5
Acts 9:40
Luke 22:41
1 Samuel 1:26

For the Romans of 46 BC, Kneeling before Caesar was a sign of surrender. Standing was a privilege. Standing to praise God is a privilege for the Baptized. For the Bible tells us that only those in Grace have the right to Stand before Him. Kneeling is the most sublime form of Adoration for the suppliant Christian.[276] During the 4th Century, some Christians began to kneel at Mass. Kneeling on Sunday, the day of the Lord's Resurrection, was reserved only for the penitent. However, at the Council of Nicaea, Turkey in 325 AD, all kneeling was forbidden. [205]

"Since there are some who kneel on Sunday and during the Season of Pentecost, this Holy Synod decrees that one should offer one's Prayers to the Lord standing."

By the end of the 5th Century, everyone knelt only during the Prayers of the Faithful petitions. [156] At the Church Synod of Tours of 813 AD, Bishops allowed parishioners to kneel in Church during Good Friday Services as a way of presenting their Prayer of Petition before God. Then, gradually, kneeling became a common posture in Mass, though there were no Kneelers in Churches before that time.

By 1022 AD, kneeling was incorporated into every Mass during the Eucharistic Prayer, and while receiving Holy Communion. This was seen as the most intense gesture of adoration and supplication to God, for it requires something sacrificial from us.[206] Both forms are sublime and valid ways to glorify God present at the Altar. [207]

WHY DO WE Hear A Eucharistic Prayer?

In it, the Priest asks the Holy Spirit to Transform the Bread and Wine into the Body and Blood of Christ.

John 2:1
Luke 22:19
1 Corinthians 11:23

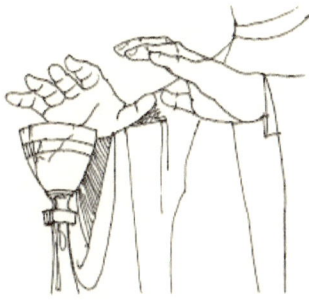

In 150 AD, the Eucharistic Prayer was kept a secret from non-baptized people. This was because it contained the Injunction of The Lord to Eat His Body and to Drink His Blood. Priests were the only ones allowed to repeat these Sacred Words. During this prayer the Holy Spirit is invoked twice, to come upon the Altar and transform the Bread and Wine. This invocation to "Call Down Upon" is called in Greek, "*Epiklesis*". [208]

Around 235 AD, St Hippolytus wrote in his Apostolic Tradition the Eucharistic Prayer we have today in daily Mass, known as the Second Eucharistic Prayer.

In 590 AD, Pope Gregory I codified the Eucharistic Prayer number One, which is used today mostly during Sunday Mass. [209]

By the 7th Century AD, the book containing the Eucharistic Prayers and Prefaces to be used at the Altar was called the "Liber Sacramentorum" or Sacramentary.

 WHY DO WE Hear Hand Bells Ring In Church?

They announce to us that the Bread and Wine are about to become the Body and Blood of Christ.

Exodus 28:33

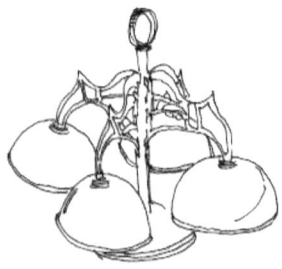

Around 380 AD, the new converts to Christianity brought with them pagan traditions, including the use of small hand bells to cast out evil spirits.[212] The Church was extremely reluctant to accept them at first. Sixth Century Celtic Missionaries adopted the use of these and larger outdoor bells to call the People to Mass. Bells were also rung three times a day to indicate when it was time to pray the Angelus, and during Funerals to let everybody know that a Spirit was being lifted up to Heaven.

By the 11th Century, the Church had begun ringing small hand bells at Mass during the Consecration of the Bread and Wine. [213] The Priest stood before the Altar, then the bells announced the pivotal moment while he blessed the Offering. After he had lifted both the Body and Blood of Christ, he genuflected to adore Him, and the bells rang again. Finally, the bells rang again three times before Communion. In Rome, a century later small bells were introduced to alert people to the approach of the Pope during Papal Processions. These sets of bells were known as the Tintinnabulum.

WHAT IS Transubstantiation?

✔ By virtue of his Ordination and the Power of the Holy Spirit, a Priest receives the Capacity to transform the Substance of the Bread and Wine into the Body and Blood of Christ.

John 6:52
Mark 14:22
Matthew 26:26
Luke 22:17
Luke 24:30

When a Priest stands before the Altar during Mass, he no longer represents himself, but Christ. Consequently, his actions imitate those of Christ too. He prays Words taken directly from the Bible. [214]

"He... takes the Bread and, holding it slightly... raises his eyes... bows lightly... and says 'Take This, All of You, and Eat of It, For This is My Body, Which Will Be Given Up For You'.

At this moment, we believe the Miracle of Transubstantiation takes place. [274]

The words for the Prayer of Consecration have remained unchanged since Christ pronounced them at His Last Supper in c29 AD. Since then, the Apostles and their Successors have proclaimed Transubstantiation to be the Summit of the Mysteries of our Faith. St Cyril, Bishop of Jerusalem in 350 AD proclaimed, [215]

"For whatever God the Holy Spirit touches is surely sanctified and changed".

The priest, after elevating the Body and Blood of Jesus, humbly places them over the altar and genuflects in adoration. [216]

For those who doubted that the Bread and Wine had become the Body and Blood of Christ, St Cyril, the Bishop of Jerusalem in 380 AD, wrote,[210]

"Since He Himself declared of the Bread, 'This Is My Body', who shall dare to doubt any longer? And since He Himself affirmed, 'This Is My Blood,' who shall ever hesitate, saying that it is not his blood? Let faith strengthen you".

WHY DO WE Pray For The Dead During The Eucharistic Prayer?

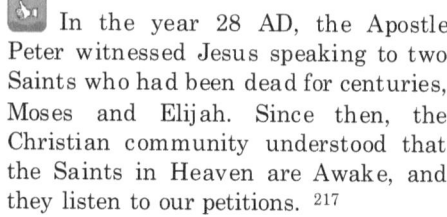 We ask God to aid those who are in Purgatory.

Luke 23:43
Mark 9:4
Luke 16:19
1 Timothy 2:5
2 Timothy 1:16
2 Maccabees 12:44

In the year 28 AD, the Apostle Peter witnessed Jesus speaking to two Saints who had been dead for centuries, Moses and Elijah. Since then, the Christian community understood that the Saints in Heaven are Awake, and they listen to our petitions. [217]

In 410 AD, Saint Augustine explained the reason for our prayers for the dead in Mass. [218]

"The souls of our beloved dead are not separated from the Church, which even now is the Kingdom of Christ; otherwise there would be no remembrance made of them at the Altar of God in the partaking of the Body of Christ."

In the 5th Century, each Church had a set of wooden boards covered in wax in which they wrote the names of the faithful departed to remind them of the need to pray for them. These tablets were called "*Diptychs*", in Greek for Two-folds. A Deacon read these out aloud when asking God to intercede for them.

? WHY DO WE Proclaim The Great Amen?

✓ We end the Eucharistic Prayer by giving all Honor and Glory to God the Trinity and we assent by chanting Amen. 219

1 Timothy 2:5
Numbers 5:1
Nehemiah 5:13
Revelation 5:14
Revelation 7:12
2 Corinthians 1:20
1 Chronicles 16:36

When a Deacon holds the Chalice, and a Priest holds the Paten chanting "*Through Him, with Him, and In Him...*" this marks the ending of the Eucharistic Prayer. We call this moment the Great Elevation. It reminds us of the Passover Meal of c29 AD when Jesus elevated the dish and cup and moved them from him to the west, from him to the east, from him to the north and south. Jews called this movement the "*Terumah*". 216

We join in by chanting AMEN, a time to stand up tall and firm giving honor and glory to God. Amen is a Hebrew word that translates in three different ways, "*So Be It!*", "*I Want That to be So*" and "*Yes, I Agree with That*". The word Amen first appears in the Bible in the Book of Numbers.

As early as 212 AD the Eucharistic Prayer ended with the sublime Prayer of Praise to God.

"*Through Him, Glory to You, and Honor to the Father and the Son, with the Holy Spirit, in Your Holy Church, Now and Forever. AMEN.*" The Church at this time began to call this Epitome of Praise The Great Amen. Saint Augustine recalls in his Sermons that the People sang The Great Amen so loudly and so strongly that he was many times worried that the roof of his Cathedral, the "*Basilica Pacis*" in Algeria might collapse. 220 Today, the Great Amen continues to be equally important to us. 221

WHY DO WE Recite The 'Our Father'?

✅ We are approaching God as our Dad. He forgives us and asks us to do the same. He is about to give us our Daily Eucharistic Bread. 222

Galatians 4:6
Luke 11:2
Matthew 4:8
Matthew 6:9
Romans 8:15

The Lord's Prayer is the most complete prayer Jesus taught his disciples, around 28 AD. In it, He asked us to call God, "*Abba*", or Dad. Because of Baptism, we are adopted children of God. In 50 AD, Jewish Converts to Christianity were accustomed to praying the "*Eighteen Benedictions*" three times per day, known as the "*Shemoneh Esreh*". 294 Once they became Catholics, they replaced those Benediction Prayers with the recitation of 18 Our Fathers, three times every day. 223

In 248 AD, Bishop Cyprian of Carthage explained the meaning of the Our Father prayer at Mass. 224

"We ask that this Bread should be given to us daily, that we who are in Christ and daily receive the Eucharist for the Food of Salvation may not be kept, by the obstacle of some heinous sin from Communion with the Heavenly Bread, and thus be separated from Christ's Body".

This prayer is so radical for it asks us to forgive others in the same way God forgives us of our debts, and sins. Until 604 AD, People prayed the Our Father immediately after the Consecration of the Body and Blood. Pope Gregory the Great placed it between the Eucharistic Prayer and the Communion instead as it is today. 225

WHY DO WE Pray 'For The Kingdom, The Power And The Glory...'?

✔ We are giving All Glory back to God and we ask Him for His Peace as we await His return.

Matthew 6:13
Titus 2:13

The document called *"Didache"* written around 60 AD added a powerful conclusion to the prayer of the Our Father. [226]

"Neither Pray ye as the hypocrites, but as the Lord hath commanded in His Gospel so pray ye .. Our Father, who art in heaven [...] but deliver us from the evil ... for Thine is the Power and the Glory, for ever, Amen".

Christians of the first 300 years continued praying the *"Didache's"* acclamation after the Lord's Prayer. This custom vanished around 350 AD, after St Cyril, Bishop of the Church in Jerusalem, mandated that after the *"Deliver us from evil, you say only: Amen".*[227]

During the 16th Century, the Phrase *"For Thine Is the Power and the Glory For Ever..."* was introduced to the Mass before the Sign of Peace, it was called the *"Embolism"*, or insertion. This was in response to the conclusion reached by Protestant Reformation scholars. For they had concluded that the Response had indeed formed part of the original Lord's Prayer in the Gospel of St Matthew.

Today, we praise God and we beg Him to send us His peace, and to protect us from all anxiety while we await His return.

"For the Kingdom the Power and the Glory are Yours now and forever". [228]

WHY DO WE Give Each Other The Sign Of Peace?

Through Baptism we are part of one family and God grants us His peace and we share it with each other.

John 20:21
Matthew 5:23
Colossians 1:20

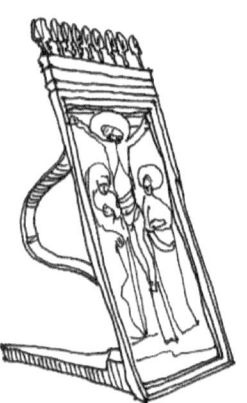

The Sign of Peace is one the four remaining Rituals from the Mass of 150 AD. In Hebrew, the word for *Peace* is "*Shalom*", meaning All Prosperity. The Sign of Peace dates from when Jesus greeted His Apostles at His Last Passover Meal and after His Resurrection by saying, "*Peace Be With You*". [229]

During the 2nd Century, St Paul encouraged a Fraternal Kiss before the Offertory in Mass, men to men, and women to women. In 417 AD, Pope Innocent I, officially moved the Fraternal Kiss or Sign of Peace before Communion. [230]

During the 6th Century, the Church in Jerusalem replaced the Kiss for a Hand Gesture. The Bishop, after asking Jesus in the Eucharist for His Peace, held his hands together in prayer as the servers solemnly wrapped their hands around his, and in turn they repeated this gesture. They passed God's peace to each member of the community. [231]

In Europe during the 12th century, the hand gesture was dropped. The new Sign of Peace was replaced by kissing a wood or metal board called in Latin, "*Pax Brede*" or Peace Board. A Priest kissed the tablet first, before passing it around the congregation. Today the gesture for the Sign of Peace throughout the world varies according to local tradition. [232]

WHY DO WE Pray 'Lamb Of God, You Take Away The Sins...'?

✓ It reminds us that Christ is the Lamb who was Sacrificed at the Altar of the Cross for our sins.

Genesis 22:6
Isaiah 53:7
John 1:29
Revelation 19:9
Exodus 29:15

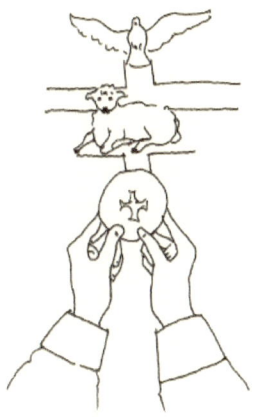

The Book of Genesis tells us that Abraham took his son Isaac to be sacrificed. God was testing his faith. As his son carried the wood up to Mount Moriah, he asked, *"Father, where is the lamb?"* Abraham's response was, *"God will provide"* in Hebrew, *"Yir'eh Salem"*. This Mount became Jerusalem. [233]

At around 500 BC, the Prophet Isaiah had seen a vision of God transformed into a Lamb that was going to die for the sins of all. During this time, if a person had committed a sin, he came to the priest, and by placing his hand on a lamb's head, his sins transferred onto the animal, then the priest slaughtered it. [303] In 26 AD, when John the Baptist saw Jesus coming towards him, he said,

"Look. This is the Lamb of God who takes away the Sins of the World".

On the night of Jesus' Last Seder Meal, they didn't have the lamb prescribed in the ritual because God was to provide the Lamb promised to Abraham. Jesus was the lamb, He died crucified on the hill of Jerusalem. [265]

The Christians of the 2nd Century regarded the Mass as the Lamb's Passover Sacrifice. In 701 AD, Pope Sergius I, decided to honor Jesus, the Lamb, by asking People to pray three times *"Lamb of God, Who Takes Away the Sins of the World have Mercy on Us"*, after the Sign of Peace. He finished the prayer with *"Grant us peace"*. Concomitantly the priest breaks the Eucharistic Bread into multiple pieces for Communion.

 **WHY DO WE See The Celebrant Break the Host Over the Chalice?**

✔ To symbolize Christ's violent death on the Cross, and that the Blood comes from His Wounded Body.234

▶ Luke 22:19
Luke 24:30

📖 This tradition dates back to c29 AD, when Jesus, at his Last Passover Meal, broke the Bread, saying, "*This is My Body*". Then He gave it to His disciples to eat and partake of Communion with Him. The Bible says that after his Resurrection, two of his disciples didn't recognize him until after he broke the Bread with them. 174

By the 2nd Century, the Host was broken over the Chalice in four parts. One part was placed inside the Chalice, the second part was consumed by the Priest. The third was reserved for the Deacon to take to another Church as a sign of unity. The largest part was given to the people for Communion. 235 By the 8th Century, Bishops broke the Host in three parts and made the Sign of the Cross over the Chalice while holding the first part with their left hand.

 **WHY DO WE See Priests Dip A Piece Of The Host Inside The Chalice?**

✓ This is the symbol for the community's unity with their Bishop, the successor of the first Apostles.

Malachi 1:11
John 17:21

This small piece of Eucharist is called the "*Fermentum*", which in Latin means to Ferment because it ferments unity. Since the first Mass of c29 AD when Jesus took the holy Bread, broke it and cast a fragment inside His Chalice, every priest had dipped the "*Fermentum*", in the Chalice to symbolize the union of Jesus' Flesh and Blood mingling together. [236]

As Christian Communities grew in numbers during the 2nd Century, it became difficult for a Bishop to visit every Church community. When the Bishop broke the Eucharistic Bread in Mass, he kept one piece aside for a Deacon to take to another Community Church under the care of his Priests, this came to be known as a Parish. Upon receiving this "*Fermentum*", the Priest dropped it into a Chalice containing the Blood of Christ to symbolize his union with his Bishop and the entire Church.

WHY DO WE Pray 'Lord, I Am Not Worthy That You Should Enter...'?

God is about to come into our bodies and hearts, so we become aware of it and humble ourselves.

Matthew 8:8
Luke 7:7
John 2:14
Numbers 21:8

When a Priest says *"Blessed are Those Called to the Supper of the Lamb"*, he asks us to become aware of the Sacredness of receiving Holy Communion. We then respond with the words the Roman Centurion spoke to Jesus asking Him to Cure his servant,

"Lord, I am not worthy that You should enter under my roof, but only say a word and my servant shall be healed" [237]

Moses lifted up a serpent in the desert on a pole, and those who looked at it were saved from dying. In the same way, the 2nd Century Christians saw Jesus in the Eucharist being lifted up on the Cross, for them to be healed from sin. This is the reason why we see the symbol of a snake on a pole in many healthcare facilities.

The first account we have of a response from the people before Communion, dates back to 350 AD, when the Bishop of Jerusalem, St Cyril asked his priests to add the invitation, [238]

"Holy things for the Holy", People standing were to respond, *"One is Holy, One is the Lord, Jesus Christ"*.

Then St Cyril wrote to all the Baptized in Jerusalem,

"Holy are you too, who have been found worthy of the Holy Spirit, to receive the Holy One...Never cut yourselves off from Communion; never let yourselves be deprived, through the pollution of sin".

WHY DO WE Fast Before Receiving Holy Communion?

Is not a wafer that we eat but the Body of Jesus, and thus we abstain from food or liquids for one hour.

Luke 2:37
Matthew 6:16
Acts 13:2
1 Corinthians 7:1

First Century converts from Judaism had followed two forms of Fasting, namely Minor Fasting and Complete Abstinence. The first one involved abstaining from wearing jewelry or makeup, and not taking food and drink from sunset to dinnertime at 3 pm the following day. The second one was similar to the Minor Fasting plus abstaining from sexual intercourse. For them, the soul and the body complemented each other, meaning that when the body abstained from its needs, the soul gained in its beauty before God.

In 60 AD, the Church asked to have two memorial Fasting days, Wednesday and Friday, the day the Lord died. The Friday Fast lasted for forty hours before receiving Holy Communion. In 303 AD, Bishops at the Council of Hippo mandated that only those who Fasted could receive Communion. The reason: 239

"It has pleased the Holy Ghost that, to honor so great a Sacrament, the Lord's Body should enter the mouth of the Christian before other food".

Pope Pius XII in 1957 modified the *Fast* to three-hours for food and one for liquids. In 1964, Pope Paul VI changed the *Fast* just one hour before Holy Communion and that neither medicines or water break the Fast.

WHY DO WE Receive Communion kneeling or Standing?

 Our bodies reflect the disposition of our spirit, if we kneel we are Humble Servants before our Lord; if we stand we are Prepared Soldiers before our King.

Exodus 29:32

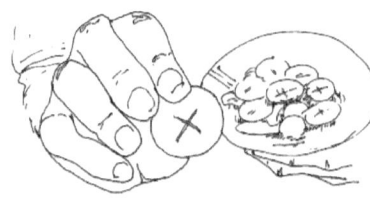

The word Communion comes from the Greek, "*Koinonia*" meaning Sharing Unity. By receiving Holy Communion, we share the Life of God. From 313 AD onward, only the Baptized came forward in the form of a Procession to receive the Body of Christ in their hands, after genuflecting. 240

In 315 AD, St Cyril was first to set in writing the way a Soldier of Christ receives Communion. 241

"In approaching, do not come forward with your wrists apart or your fingers spread. Make your left hand a Throne for the right since you are receiving into it a King, and cup your hand and receive the Body of Christ and say 'Amen'."

By 480 AD Pope Gelasius I, declared that it had become compulsory to stand while receiving Communion. Around the year 1000 AD, The Church saw kneeling to receive Communion on the tongue as the most intense Gesture of Adoration before our Lord. 242 In 1965, the Church allowed both forms to receive Communion, though emphasized receiving it while kneeling. In 2011, the Church reminded Catholics that God is who we receive in Communion, therefore, those who stand should genuflect or bow before receiving the Blessed Body and Blood of Christ.

WHY DO WE Receive Both The Body And Blood Of Christ?

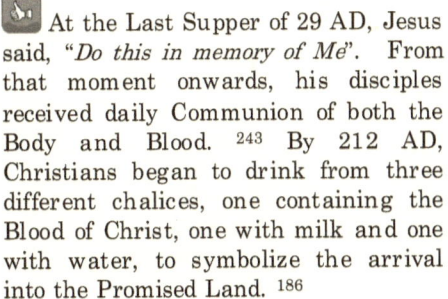 Jesus said, unless you Eat my Body and Drink my Blood, you will not have life eternal.

John 6:8
Acts 2:46

At the Last Supper of 29 AD, Jesus said, "*Do this in memory of Me*". From that moment onwards, his disciples received daily Communion of both the Body and Blood. [243] By 212 AD, Christians began to drink from three different chalices, one containing the Blood of Christ, one with milk and one with water, to symbolize the arrival into the Promised Land. [186]

Around the year 500 AD, Holy Communion was about receiving only the Body of Christ on Sundays. By the end of the 800's AD, people abstained from Sunday Communion altogether as they felt unworthy. Only the priest received often.

In 1216 AD, at the Fourth Lateran Council, Pope Innocent III mandated Communion of the Body of Christ at least once a year. The Council of Trent, in 1555 AD, encouraged frequent Communion of the Body of Christ. In 1905 AD, Pope Pius X encouraged Communion of the Body to be taken as often as once a day. Next, in 1965, the Blood was added back into Communion just like the 2nd Century Christians did. Pope Paul VI allowed us to receive Holy Communion up to twice per day.

If we receive only the Bread, but not the Blood at Communion, we still receive the full Person of Christ, even if it is a single Drop or Crumb.

WHY DO Christians Of Other Faiths Not Receive Holy Communion?

 To receive Jesus, one must have fasted one hour before, confessed their sins, believe that Jesus is truly in the Eucharist, and should be in union with the local bishop and the Pope.

1 Corinthians 10:16

When people go out dining at a five star restaurant, they normally have to make reservations in advance, dress up nicely and bring enough cash to pay for their meal. In a similar way, when we come to the Banquet of Communion, we are required to Fast for at least one hour, have confessed all Grave Sins, to Believe that Jesus is really present in the Holy Eucharist, and to be in Communion with the Local Bishop, and the Pope. This is why a person who may follow Christ, but is not part of our Faith, does not receive Communion at Mass.

Christians from the 2nd Century onwards made sure that only those properly Baptized and prepared to receive the Eucharist stayed on for Holy Communion. 244

"No-one is allowed to Partake of it except Those who Believe that Our Teachings are True, and who have been Cleansed in the Bath for the Forgiveness of Sins".

Since 1965, the Church has allowed People of other Faiths to stay throughout Mass. Although they don't receive Communion, they can still come forward, fold their arms in the shape of an "X" instead, and receive a Blessing from the Priest or Minister. However, this Blessing is optional, since at the end of Mass everyone receives a final Blessing from the priest.

 WHY DO WE Say Amen after receiving the Body and Blood?

✓ By saying Amen we assent, Yes it is true, it is the Body of Christ.

Exodus 29:38

During the first Mass in c29 AD, Jesus gave His Body and Blood to His Apostles, yet their silence reflected their lack of understanding of what they were receiving. After His Resurrection, we only know they prayed in silence as they received Communion.

By 315 AD, we know Christians were saying Amen after receiving Holy Communion. St Cyril of Jerusalem says that after we receive the Blood of Christ we respond, Amen, and while the moisture is still upon our lips, we should touch it with our hands, and bless our eyes and forehead and the other organs of sense for having witnessed God. [245]

In 418 AD, St Augustine explained the meaning of the Amen, [246]

"For you hear the words "The Body of Christ" and respond 'Amen' – 'Yes it is true! Be, then, a member of the Body of Christ, that your 'Amen' may be true."

WHY DO
WE See In
Some
Churches
Communion
Rails?

These rails facilitate the reception of Holy Communion while kneeling.

Ezra 9:5
Daniel 6:10
Luke 22:41
Mark 1:40

By the end of the 8th Century, people ceased bringing produce and other foods as gifts for the Offertory. The Altar Side Tables became ledges. Their function served to separate the Sanctuary from the Nave of the Church and to distribute Holy Communion. In the Churches of Byzantium, the Altar Rail soon took the form of a high screen to hang icons, for people to kiss. [77] This wall was known as the "*Iconostasis*", reminiscent of the tall curtain at the entrance of the Holy of Holies in the Jewish Temple of Jerusalem. [25]

In Rome during 1614 AD, the Church decided that these ledges should be transformed into Communion Rails where People could kneel to receive Holy Communion.

During Vatican II in 1965, the Church decided to return to the style of 4th Century Processions, and this is why most People now receive Holy Communion standing. However, the Church continues to encourage the reception of Holy Communion while kneeling on Communion Rails. [247]

WHY DO Ministers Place The Eucharist Inside A Small Receptacle?

✔ The Eucharistic Bread is taken to the ill, the infirm and the elderly for Communion inside a Pyx.

📖 Hebrews 9:4
Exodus 16:4
John 6:32

👍 The *"Pyx"* is a Greek word for Box. When 2nd Century Christians celebrated the Eucharistic sacrifice in their homes, they kept the Holy Bread inside a wooden or metal Pyx. By the 4th Century, people no longer kept the Eucharist in their homes and so Jesus in the Eucharistic Bread dwelled inside a Pyx in Church and from here it was taken to the infirm and elderly. [248]

During this time, Priests hid the Pyx inside a column or in the Sacristy of the Church in order to protect the Eucharist from desecration by invaders. By the 7th Century, the expanding Church needed a larger receptacle locked by a key where a Pyx and ciborium could be placed. This became known as the Tabernacle.

WHAT IS A Tabernacle?

 This is God's dwelling Place in Church. It holds the Pyx, and Ciborium containing the Blessed Eucharist. We genuflect before it.

Exodus 29:44
John 1:14
John 6:50
Revelation 21:3

Tabernacle or "*Mishkan*" in Hebrew means large tent or dwelling place. Around 1450 BC, God fed His people with bread from Heaven called Manna. God then directed Moses to build Him a dwelling place among His people, where a jar containing Manna was to be kept at all times.

For 2nd Century Christians, the Eucharist was their Bread from Heaven. God's dwelling place was in their homes inside a Pyx. During the 7th Century, the expanding community needed a much larger receptacle locked by a key inside their Church. This became known as the Tabernacle. This receptacle was kept away from the public view inside the Sacristy.

During the Synod of Cologne, in 1281 AD, Bishops requested Pope Martin IV for permission to display the Tabernacle outside the Sacristy, and to allow its elevation above the Altars. This was the first time that all Tabernacles were visible in Churches, and available for the adoration of the Eucharistic Lord by all. Today, the Church reminds us that the Tabernacle should be located in an especially worthy place in Church, in a way that manifests the truth of the real presence of Jesus in the Eucharistic Bread. 249

WHY DO WE See A Red Lamp Lit Next To The Tabernacle?

✓ The Sanctuary Lamp burns constantly as a reminder of God's Presence in the Blessed Eucharist.

Exodus 27:20

The inner shrine of the Jewish Tabernacle of the year 1450 BC, contained the Ark of the Covenant.[269] Within which the tablets of the Ten Commandments, the rod of Aaron and the jar with Manna rested. The outer chamber housed the Golden Lampstand with seven lights that burnt continuously before God as a Symbol of His presence. This Lamp reminded people of the seven days of God's creation. [250]

In 1246 AD, at the Feast of Corpus Christi, the Bishops of England imitated the Jewish ritual of the Golden Lampstand and began to burn a constant light next to the Tabernacle in all their Churches. Later, in 1545 AD, at the Council of Trent, this practice was made obligatory everywhere. Today, if we walk into a Church and would like to know where the Tabernacle is located, we look for the eternal ruby colored flame called the Sanctuary Lamp. [251]

WHY DO Deacons Pour Water Inside The Chalice After Communion?

He purifies them to make sure no fragments from the Blessed Eucharist remain in them.

Leviticus 6:28
Matthew 23:25
1 Corinthians 4;16

A Priest or Deacon purifies the holy vessels by pouring water into them. After that, he drinks the water and wipes the vessels clean with a Purificator. This ritual dates back to around 400 AD. At this time, Bishop John Chrysostom directed his Priests to drink some water or to eat a piece of bread after administering Communion. This ritual, called the Ablution of the Mouth, ensured that no Eucharistic Bread or Blood remained in their mouths. Later, a sip of unconsecrated wine served the same purpose.

Around the 13th Century, the Church linked the Ablution of the Mouth to the washing of the Chalice and purification of the celebrant's hands after Communion. The prayers during the Ablution took place at first in silence. Much later the prayer was added, 252

"A pure mind is a Holy Temple for God, and a Heart clean and without sin is His Best Altar".

By 1570 AD, Pope Pius V had codified the ritual prayers and actions for this part of Mass, and we use them to this day. 253

WHY DO WE Hear A Final Blessing During the Dismissal?

✓ We need the Favor of God as we go forth into our daily lives, and live worthy of the Mysteries we just experienced. 255

Leviticus 9:22
Luke 24:50

The first priest in the Bible to give a blessing to his people was Aaron, around 1200 BC. Jews called it the *"Cohanim Blessing"* because God's grace flows through the hands of the priest onto the people. 280

In 29 AD, Jesus lifted his hands and blessed his disciples before his Ascension into Heaven. Since then, a priest has blessed his people during the Dismissal at Mass.

In 215 AD, Saint Hippolytus was the first Christian to mention the Dismissal at Mass. 254

"Let the Bishop say: The Lord be with You... Let the People reply: And with Your Spirit... Let the Deacon say: Go in Peace. With that, the Sacrifice is Ended."

By 500 AD, many Churches ended their Masses with a Silent Blessings or none at all. At other times, these ended with a simple invitation

"Let us Bless the Lord".

By the year 700, AD Pope St Sergius I began to bless the people in silence as he processed out of Church. During the 13th Century, the prayer for Blessings once again emerged. In 1570 AD, Pope St Pius V codified the text for the Blessing as it is today,

"Go forth, the Mass is Ended".

The minister, acting in the person of Christ, extends his anointed hands and imparts God's blessing to us, in the name of the Father, Son and Holy Spirit. 256

WHY DO WE Have Eucharistic Adoration?

This is private time to spend with Jesus in the Blessed Eucharist.

Philippians 2:10
Acts 4:12
Matthew 28:19

In 1246 AD, the Church decided to authoritatively clarify the doctrine of the real presence of Jesus in the Eucharistic Bread. To reinforce this, Pope Celestine IV declared a new feast day named the Body of Christ, in Latin, "*Corpus Christi*".

Devotion to the Eucharist flourished as people came to Church during the day or night to adore Jesus in the Eucharist for hours. People began to report miracles happening to them, and the fervor increased.

Today, we adore Jesus at daily Mass, when we read Holy Scripture and in Eucharistic Adoration. In some Churches, the Adoration Chapel is a side room to the nave adorned with flowers, candles, a Sanctuary Lamp, and the Tabernacle.

When a Minister presents the Eucharistic Bread for adoration, this is called the Exposition. We genuflect as we enter the chapel, after which we may either sit or kneel. This is the perfect time for personal dialogue with Jesus, for praying the Rosary, or for meditation.

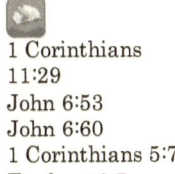 **WHAT DOES IT Mean That Jesus Is Present In The Eucharist?**

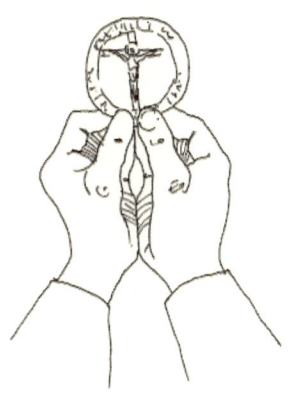 It means that He decided to Stay with us in the form of Bread so we can consume Him and Live His Life.

1 Corinthians 11:29
John 6:53
John 6:60
1 Corinthians 5:7
Exodus 12:7

There is no doubt that the Church of 29 AD regarded Jesus' Words, *"This is My Body"* as real. They didn't think it was a metaphor or an image. After all, Jesus Is God and whatever He says, it happens. In a manuscript from 160 AD, Justin the Martyr wrote. [257]

"We call this Food the 'Eucharist'. No one is allowed to Partake of it except Those who Believe that Our Teachings are True, and who have been Cleansed in the Bath for the Forgiveness of Sins".

"Not as common bread or as common drink do we receive these. But just as through the Word of God Jesus Christ our Savior became Incarnate and Took Flesh and Blood for our Salvation, so we have been taught that the Food over which Thanks has been given by the Prayers of his Word, and which nourishes our flesh and blood by Assimilation, is both the Flesh and Blood of that Incarnate Jesus".

In 304 AD, Emperor Diocletian killed 49 Christians because of their refusal to renounce their faith in the Holy Eucharist. They are known as the Martyrs of Abitina. [275]

Around 829 AD, the first monks who doubted Jesus' real presence in the Eucharist were abbot Paschasius Radbertus and monk, Ratramnus. By 1065 AD, the debate got intensified when two other monks became vocal, Berengarius of Tours and abbot Lanfranc, of a monastery in Normandy. The debate came to an end in 1216 AD, at the Fourth Lateran Council, when Pope Innocent III, declared,

"In the Sacrament of the Altar, under the species of bread and wine, his Body and Blood are truly contained, the bread having been transubstantiated into his Body and the wine into his Blood by the divine power".

 WHY DO WE See A Monstrance On The Altar When There Is No Mass?

✅ This vessel displays Jesus publicly in the Eucharistic Bread for everyone to Adore.

1 John 3:16
Revelation 19:10

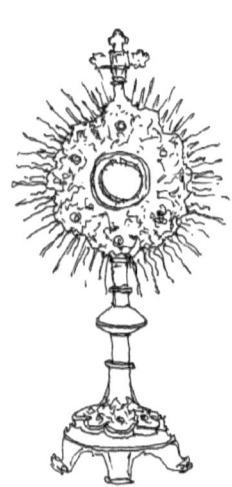

📢 "*Monstrance*" in Latin means to Demonstrate. For 2nd Century Christians, there was no need to display the Body of Christ for adoration because they took it home with them for the Communion of the sick and dying. After 325 AD, however, the Blessed Eucharistic Bread remained in a secret place inside each Church.

During the 9th Century, Bishops began to carry the Eucharist with them inside a covered Ciborium in processions, and thus a new tradition began. As the Eucharistic Bread was replaced by Hosts made by Monks, and the round shape became the norm, a new type of Ciborium was needed; a larger and more practical vessel in which to carry the Blessed Eucharist in procession. 258

In 1246 AD, the Feast of Corpus Christi was instituted, and soon after this new cylindrically shaped Ciborium appeared. The Monstrance was made of gold or silver and adorned with precious stones. At the top of it, the Blessed Sacrament was visible through a rounded glass called the Lunette. After processing through the city streets, the Bishop and his people arrived at Church. Here, everyone remained kneeling in adoration until they received a blessing. This was known as Benediction.

Part Three

AS WE GO FORTH

? WHY IS THE Mass The Highest Form Of Prayer?

✓ Our Faith and every Prayer are founded in the Crucifixion and Resurrection of Jesus, which is the Mass.

Acts 2:42
John 3:16
Galatians 2:20
1 Corinthians 15:17

Mass is the Celebration that renews the Lord's Last Supper, His Sacrifice on the Cross, and His Resurrection. This is our Central Act of Worship. For if Jesus had Died and not Resurrected, our Faith would be in vain, for we would still be in sin; that's what the Bible says.

Around 29 AD, After the Apostles received the Holy Spirit at Pentecost, they devoted themselves to pray Mass. Prayer in Latin is "*Precarious*" meaning to Obtain. For anyone to obtain God's gift of Eternal Life, God had to Send His Only Son to Die on the Cross in ransom for sin.

Mass is more than a ritual, it is the reliving of Jesus' Crucifixion, Death and Resurrection. He Feeds His people with His Flesh and Blood. Therefore, the Mass is the highest form of prayer. It is because of His Sacrifice on the Cross that we become His Adoptive Children and only then do we have the privilege to call God,

"Our Father, who art in Heaven..."

WHERE DOES THE Term 'Mass' Come From?

Mass comes from the Latin word "*Missa*" meaning Dismissal.

John 19:30

Greek was the official language of the Church until 384 AD, when Pope Damasus I changed it to Latin so that everyone could better understand their Faith. When the Liturgy was translated from Greek to Latin, the Church needed a new name for the Eucharistic Sacrifice. We know that Bishop Ambrose of Milan used the word "*Mass*" in 386 AD for the first time when he wrote a letter in Latin to his sister telling her how he managed to celebrate the "*Missa*" or the Mass, despite the rioting in Milan.

Soon after this time, Deacons began to chant in Latin at the end of the Eucharistic Celebration "*Ite Missa Est*" meaning, "*Go, it is Finished*" or "*Go, you are Dismissed*". The People of the 4th Century began to refer to the Liturgy as the "*Dismissal*" or the "*Sent Forth.*" Today, we simply call it the Mass.

WHY DON'T WE Find The Word Mass In The Bible?

✓ The New Testament Books were written in Greek, not in Latin, therefore they used the terms "Breaking of the Bread" or the "Agapai Meal" instead.

Acts 2:42
Luke 22:19
Jude 1:12
Colossians 3:17
1 Thessalonians 5:18

Mass was said in the Greek language during the first three Centuries. Christians called the Mass by many names including "*Eucharistein*", or the Giving Thanks, and the "*Agapai*" or Agape Meal. Other Communities called it The Sacrifice Service, others The Offering Service, and yet others The Liturgy meaning the Public Work of the People. However, the most common name found in the Bible is the Breaking of the Bread, or *"Klasei tou Artou"* in Greek.

St Paul, writing to the Church in Thessalonica, reminded them about God's Will for every Christian:

"In everything you do, Give Thanks [Eucharistete], for this is the Will of God for you!"

WHAT IS THE Origin Of The Mass?

 Jesus chose the Jewish Passover as His Last Supper. That night, He became the Lamb that was Sacrificed and Eaten to free His people from slavery of sin.

Exodus 12:11
Leviticus 23:5
Exodus 13:7
Exodus 13:10
1 Corinthians 11:24

The Passover or Seder Meal remembers God freeing His People from slavery in Egypt around 1400 BC. That night, God sent His Angel to kill the first-born baby of every household that had not eaten a lamb and posted some of its blood on the door lintel. The next morning, Pharaoh feared God and allowed his Jewish slaves to go away.

Up to the year 29 AD, no person had ever dared to add his own rituals to this Sacred Feast. On that night, though, Jesus added His Own Words, which were to mark the beginning of His Own Passover.

"*Take and eat, this is My Body, which is being Broken for You*".

Next, He gave Thanks to God, Broke the Bread and gave it to His Disciples to Eat. In Greek, the word for Giving Thanks is "*Eucharistein*".

Then, He took the large Cup of Wine called "*Mezrak*", saying,

"*This is My Blood which will be poured over You*".

Mass was not yet over though. Jesus, as the Lamb of God, had yet to consummate His Sacrifice by dying on the Cross and Resurrecting three days later.

For the Jewish Passover, God commanded His people to "*observe this day every year in its memory*". For Jesus' Passover God simply said, "*Do this in My Memory*".

WHY ARE 'Priest' and 'Victim' Important Concepts?

✔ There is no Sacrifice without the two. Jesus became both Lamb and Priest, and He offered Himself for us at the Altar.

Hebrews 8:1
Hebrews 10:11
Hebrews 7:24
1 John 2:1
1 Corinthians 5:7

Around the year 1400 BC, outside the Jewish Tabernacle stood a massive grill where Priests sacrificially slaughtered animals and offered them to God. They called this the Altar of Sacrifice. In this context, there were two elements important to every Sacrifice: a Priest and a Victim. For without either, the Sacrifice was impossible.

A Priest was a person chosen from among God's People to offer Sacrifice. A Victim was a pigeon or lamb chosen to represent the person who presented it to the Priest. The Priest blessed the Victim then offered it to God in Thanksgiving, or in Reparation for that Person's Sin. [303] Until 29 AD, no Jewish Priest had ever offered himself as Victim for the Sacrifice. Jesus became the first Combined Priest and Victim when He suffered Death by Crucifixion. From that moment onwards, the Priesthood changed, radically and irrevocably.

When a Priest says, *"This is My Body..."* while holding Bread, he represents that Same Christ who spoke those Words at the Last Supper. At this moment, he becomes both Priest and Victim. Vatican II taught us that, by virtue of our Baptism, we share in the Priesthood of Christ, but without the power of bringing His Body and Blood to the Altar. This means that every Baptized man or woman is a Priest and a Victim. When we come to Mass, we present ourselves as an Offering to God. [259]

WHY IS Sunday The Day Of The Lord?

Because Jesus sanctified *Sunday* when He Resurrected on that day.

Acts 20:7
Revelation 1:10
1 Corinthians 15:4

After Jesus' Resurrection, the disciples gathered to Commemorate His Sacrifice in the Mass. At first, they did this daily. Then, they did this once a year on the Feast of the Jewish Passover. Later, the Church decided it should be on every Sunday. The *"Didache"* document, dating from 60 AD, referred to this Holy Day as:

"the Day of the Lord to Come Together and Break Bread and Give Thanks [Eucharistein]".

At this time, a day started at sunset and ended at sunset, not at midnight. At sundown on Saturday, Christians congregated for Mass in a private home, for it was already Sunday. At first, Mass was a combination of a potluck known as the Agape Meal, followed by Fellowship, Prayers, Scripture Reading and then the Eucharistic Sacrifice.

By 150 AD, Bishops separated the Sunday Agape Meal from the Eucharistic Sacrifice and introduced a Fasting before the latter.

In 165 AD, Pope St Anicetus declared Sunday as officially the *"The Lord's Day"*, in Latin *"Dies Domenica,"* in Memory of His Resurrection. This was a difficult time for many to keep holy since it was the first day of the week, and a day of work just as Mondays are for us today. On March 3, 321 AD, Emperor Constantine resolved the tension by decreeing that Sunday would be the day of rest for everyone in the Roman Empire. 260

WHAT DO WE Mean By 'Sacrament' When We Talk About The Mass?

During Mass, God's Invisible Power is active through the Visible Bread and Wine, and in the words and intention of the Priest, that it may become the Body and Blood of Christ.

Psalm 84:11
John 3:5
Acts 8:14
John 6:51
John 20:21
Matthew 19:4
James 5:14
1 Corinthians 19:23

The Church defined a Sacrament as an efficacious Visible Sign containing an Invisible Reality by which Divine Life is dispensed to us, necessary for having Eternal Life. That Invisible Reality is called God's Grace.

In 212 BC, the Island of Syracuse was under siege by Roman ships. The island's army general ordered his soldiers to polish their shields for hours until they shone like bright mirrors. Then, during the attack, the shields deflected the powerful Mediterranean sun onto the Roman's ship sails, setting them on fire from 100 feet away. This power to deflect the sun's rays off the army shields onto burning sails was called in Greek *"Mysterion"* and translated in Latin as *"Sacramentum"*. The Church adopted this concept for a powerful hidden reality impossible for the naked eye to see, and visible only in its effects necessary for having Life Eternal. This power is God's own action when it comes in contact with people's hearts and souls. This was how the Christians of the 2nd Century understood the Mass as a Sacrament. Our souls are like the ship sails that are burnt with God's fire coming from the actions at Mass.

In 1216 AD, at the Fourth Lateran Council, the Church officially declared there are Seven Sacraments. These are Baptism, Confirmation, Eucharist, Reconciliation, Anointing of the Sick, Marriage and Holy Orders. We call the Eucharist the Most Blessed, Sacrament because is the Sacrament of Sacraments.

? WHAT DOES IT Mean That The Mass Is God's Eternal Time?

✓ Though Jesus' Sacrifice happened once in c29 AD, in Heaven it is happening Now in an unbloody manner.

Revelation 5:9
Acts 1:7
2 Corinthians 6:1
Luke 9:28
Hebrews 9:25
Hebrews 8:3

Time for God is neither past nor future, but only present in the now. The Church sees the Sacrifice of Jesus on the Cross as being constantly re-enacted at Altars all around the World, while also current in God's Eternal Present Time. This does not mean Jesus is being crucified over and over.

When the Christians of the 2nd Century were at Mass, they knew they were immersed into God's Eternal Time called "*Kairos*". As human beings, we experience time as "*Kronos*" that is linear time that has a past, a present and a future. For God, however, time is "*Kairos*". With all due respect, imagine God standing in the middle of a large donut pool float, while all around the float are written historic dates with people's names and events that happened and are about to happen, God sees all of them as present Now. That is "*Kairos*".

When Jesus commanded the Church at His Last Supper, in c29 AD, to "*Do this in Memory of Me*", that was a Window into God's "*Kairos*". During the Feast of Corpus Christi, on June 11, 2009, Pope Benedict XVI described "*Kairos*"

"With the Eucharist, Heaven comes down to Earth, God's Tomorrow descends into the Present Moment, and Time is, as it were Embraced by Divine Eternity".

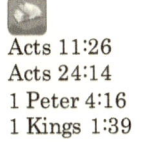 WHAT DO WE Mean By The Word 'Christian'?

✓ Those who Follow the Anointed One of God.

Acts 11:26
Acts 24:14
1 Peter 4:16
1 Kings 1:39
John 1:41
Matthew 16:16

The Romans of the 2nd Century saw Christians as no more than a Hebrew sect, which they called "*Hodon*" or The Way. The majority of Jews, though, saw them as followers of Jesus of Nazareth and referred to them as Nazarenes. Decades after Jesus' resurrection in c29 AD, the Nazarenes began their expansion into foreign lands that stretched as far afield as Turkey and Northern Africa.

When these Nazarenes reached the City of Antioch in Syria, in c44 AD, they found that the people there worshiped multiple gods and mainly spoke Greek. To their surprise, these people were not waiting for any Messiah nor did they understand its meaning.

As Nazarenes began to seek ways to explain their Faith in Jesus in terms of Greek thinking, they noticed that these people smeared their wrestlers with perfumed oils, both to emphasize their divinity, and to frustrate their opponents. The Nazarenes applied their minds to the concept of "*Anoint*". The word for "*Anointed One of God*" in Greek is "*Xristos*". This concept helped them explain that Jesus is the Christ who saves everybody from their infirmities by granting them Eternal Life. It was in this city that, for the first time, the Nazarenes were called "*Xristianous*" translated as the "*Anointedians*".

WHAT DO WE Mean By The Word 'Catholic'?

It means Universal, as in for everybody, and it also means acceptance of the Complete Teachings given by Jesus to His Church.

Acts 9:31

After the Nazarenes had adopted the term *"Christian"* in c44 AD, their faith spread rapidly among the Greeks. As these converts learned the Mysteries, many of them became Saints and Martyrs. Others, however, misinterpreted the Mysteries, taking only the teachings that they liked or mixing them with their earlier beliefs.

The Church needed a new title that would identify the True Followers of Jesus, and confirm that they were faithful to His Whole Teaching. Around 110 AD in Syria, St Ignatius, Bishop of Antioch, proposed a new concept, namely *"Katholikos"*. The word Catholic comes from the two Greek words *"Katha"* and *"Holos"* meaning *"Regarding the Whole"*. The original meaning behind this concept was Belief in the Whole Teachings of Christ and of His Church.

By 325 AD, Christians everywhere had begun using the term Catholic. That same year, St Cyril of Jerusalem told his Parishioners that whenever they entered a new town, they should not ask where the Christians gathered, but rather where the Catholics met. In 347 AD, the Church adopted a second, broader meaning to the word *"Catholic"* as the *"Universal Church"*. As St Cyril of Jerusalem explained, [293]

"It is called Catholic because it is throughout the world, from one end of the earth to the other".

WHY DO WE Celebrate Christmas On December 25th?

✓ Because it marks the day the sun begins to climb back into the sky as its new birth. For us, it marks the birth of the Son of God, Jesus.

Luke 2:1
Matthew 1:18
Isaiah 7:14
Genesis 3:15
Isaiah 11:1
Micah 5:2
Jeremiah 31:15
Matthew 2:2

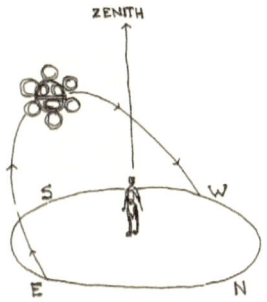

First Century Romans practiced a sun cult. They would gather at dawn to stand facing east towards the rising sun, while they prayed to their sun god, *"Sol Invictus"*. To best honor their deity, they celebrated the Winter Solstice after the sun had passed its lowest point on December 25th, and had once again begun to climb into the sky as days began to lengthen. The seven days leading to this feast day was known as the Saturnalia festivities. [282]

By the year 336 AD, Christians had transformed the feast of the birth of a sun god into the Feast of the Birth of the Son of God, Jesus Christ, named *"Natalis Invicti"*. [261] By the 5th Century, the Bishops were saying Mass on every December 25th to celebrate the Birth of the Lord, and thus nine months previous, March 25th, was the feast of Mary's Annunciation, which coincided with the Vernal Equinox.

The Christians of Alexandria, Egypt, adopted a slightly different Christmas Calendar. They chose to celebrate the Birth of Christ on January 6th instead, in order to replace an ancient Egyptian celebration of the birth of Osiris.

Germans celebrated the Feast of Yule, or Feast of Lights. They placed candles on their windows on the form of a pyramid to honor the rebirth of their deities. By 1100 AD, troubadours acted the Bible story of Adam and Eve every December 24. On stage, they displayed the *"Tree of Paradise"* decorated with apples, Yule candles and evergreens.[277] This tree became the Christmas Tree.

WHY DO We Receive Ashes On Ash Wednesday?

This marks the beginning of Lent; 40 days of preparation before Jesus' Resurrection.

Jonas 3:5
Matthew 11:21
Genesis 3:19
Mark 1:15

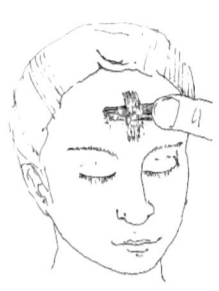

The Christians of the 2nd Century were mainly concerned with celebrating the day that Christ Resurrected, namely Easter Sunday. In order to recall the Lord's suffering, the Church instituted a new tradition in 350 AD called the Forty Day Fast in Latin, "*Quadragesima*" from where we get the word Quarantine. These were forty days set aside to relive the forty nights Jesus spent in isolation in the desert fasting and praying.

During the Forty Day Fast, Christians and those candidates for Baptism did daily public penance for their sins, except for Sundays. They ate vegan meals. Because eggs and milk were forbidden, these Christians came up with a new bread shaped in the form of little arms crossed in prayer, made with flour, salt and water, called in Latin, "*Bracellae*", translated in German "*Bretzel*"; we know it as Pretzels. If we count 40 days back from Easter Vigil, not counting Sundays, the 40th day falls on a Wednesday, or Ash Wednesday.

We have continued to celebrate this Ash Wednesday through the years. On that day, Penitents knelt and received a blessing by the Bishop in which he placed ashes on their heads as a reminder that their bodies turn into ashes when they die, but not their souls if they turned away from sin. These blessed ashes come from burned palms from the previous year's Palm Sunday feast.

WHY DO We Pray The Rosary?

The Rosary is a chain of prayer, the best way to praise the Blessed Virgin Mary. We pray it because she is our mother, who intercedes for us before her son Jesus.

Luke 1:28
Luke 1:42
1 Thessalonians 5:17

In 311 AD, St Anthony of Egypt, moved to the desert to become the first monk to pray in solitude. There, he prayed 54 Our Fathers per day. To make it easy to count prayers, he tied 54 knots around a rope, which came to be known as the Chotki rope. [223]

A story tell us that St Anthony was praying in the desert while the devil kept untying the knots on his Chotki, and St Anthony became upset. The Blessed Mother appeared and asked the saint to make a cross from the same rope so the devil would stay away.

By 431 AD, devotion to the Blessed Mother became strong when the Church declared her the Mother of God. [283] Later in the 553 AD she was declared ever Virgin. [284]

During the 8th Century, all monks at the Monastery of Cluny in France used the Chotki rope though they called it in Latin, "Paternoster" since they used it to count the Lord's Prayer. It was not until 1100 AD when the Church composed a prayer from the Gospel of St Luke known as the Hail Mary that soon the Chotki or Paternoster beads were used to count Hail Marys. [285]

In 1214 AD, the Blessed Mother appeared and asked St Dominic to promote the praying of 50 to 150 Hail Marys that came to be known as Mary's Rose Garden or Rosary Prayer. By the year 1489 AD, the 15 decades of Hail Marys separated by 15 Our Fathers had become known as Mysteries. [286]

⊙ WHY DO WE Believe in Purgatory?

✔ Purgatory is a state, not a place for those who die and are in need of purification. For the Bible tell us that nothing unclean can enter Heaven. [288]

Revelation 21:27
1 Corinthians 3:15
2 Maccabees 12:44
James 1:14

🔊 The term "Purgatory" comes from Latin meaning to purge or cleanse. Purgatory is a Catholic term but its concept precedes Christianity. In fact, the Jews at the time of Christ prayed for the dead, for the forgiveness of their sins for eleven months. They believed the soul needed eleven months to be purified before resting. [43]

Christians of the 2nd Century AD, believed that nothing unclean entered Heaven (Revelation 21:27) for if they died while having un-repented sins they must be purified (1 Corinthians 3:15); while the living were encouraged to pray for their dead, so God may free them from their sins (2 Maccabees 12:44), but those who died with deadly sin have no chance to be purified (James 1:14). [290] Though for Christians, the concepts of Heaven and Hell as places were evident from the start, the state for the purification of the soul as a place was slow to develop. [303]

By the 4th Century AD, the concept of Purgatory evolved. The apocryphal manuscript of the Vision of Paul, began to paint a severe God who punished the souls of the un-repented departed sinners, but granted some mercy and repentance to other souls. [287]

St. Ambrose, Bishop of Milan in 397 AD speaks of a Baptismal of Fire, which stands outside the gates of Heaven to purify the souls from sin. By 1206 AD, Purgatory began to be described erroneously as a place. By 1245 AD, at the First Council of Lyons, the Church finally proclaimed Purgatory as real. [304]

NOTES

1. Because of sin, Adam and Eve were expelled from Paradise. The gateway to Paradise was blocked and protected by God's angels. Jesus, by dying on the Cross, became the Gateway into Paradise once again. (Genesis 3:24).

2. Constantine subsidized 25 public buildings, and after 327 AD, built 9 churches in Rome. We must remember that prior to 313 AD, the Christian community didn't have the right to own temples of worship. They met in private homes or cemeteries for Mass. Before the destruction of the Jewish Temple in Jerusalem in 70 AD, they attended the Temple daily and the synagogues. (Acts 2:46 and Acts 13:13) However, when they attended the Temple, they no longer offered the sacrifices of lambs. Since Christ had died there was no need for further sacrifices. The only sacrifice they remembered was Christ's at the Mass.

3. Christians since the beginning considered their souls to be the temples of God, therefore, wherever they congregated, God was among them. Once Christians acquired pagan structures, the next step was to purify them and to pray to make them worthy of the Mass. The doors were adorned with Christ's symbols. But they never forgot that each of them was a holy temple and the exterior buildings only reflected the beauty of their inner souls.

4. Raeburn Michael, 1984, *Architecture Of The Western World*, Crescent Books, London, UK, 74,75

5. The fact is that souls in Purgatory are already saved. To learn more about Purgatory turn to page 124. Also see Meagher, James L., 1906, How Christ Said The First Mass, Christian Press Association Publishing Company, New York, NY, 274.

6. This door someone can open for us, or we may open it for ourselves, but in the end, it's up to us to accept God's Grace. Dubruiel, Michael, 2002-2007, The How-to Book of the Mass: Everything You Need to Know But No One Ever Taught You, Our Sunday Visitor, Huntington, IN, 40-41.

7. St Ignatius of Antioch, Letter to the Philadelphians, 5 (From here on, the circa symbol 'c.' before a number means the approximate date).

8. The invisible world has never been so near as it is for Christians. For by receiving Baptism, they no longer were strangers in a foreign land, now they were pilgrims on their way back to the

Promise Land, Heaven. They were to be called the 'chosen', 'the called out', in Greek 'Ekklesia', or Church.

9. Before Baptism, the candidate would say, "I renounce you, Satan" then spit at the Devil. The person would be anointed with the Sacred Oil in the sign of a cross, followed by a threefold immersion in the Baptismal Pool, the laying of hands, the Lord's Prayer and kiss. Wegman Herman, 1967, Christian Worship In The East And West, A Study Guide To Liturgical History, Pueblo Publishing, New York, NY, 110.

10. Baptism for the Christians of the 4th Century meant to die and to resurrect just like Christ did. Before people were baptized, they became Catechumens, a word in Greek meaning, 'being instructed'. From the writings of Theodore Mopsuestia, Prologue to the Acts of The Apostles, The American Journal of Theology 2, 1898, 363.

11. Dues, Greg, 1992, *Catholic Customs & Traditions: A Popular Guide*, Twenty-third Publications, Mystic, CT, 188

12. Archdiocese of Sydney, 2008, *Sursum Corda This is the Mass*, Sydney, Australia, 17

13. Norwich John Julius, *The Middle Sea A History Of The Mediterranean*, 2005, Vintage Books, New York, NY, 24-25

14. Romans' genuflection consisted in lowering themselves onto the left knee until it touched the floor, while bending the head forward. This gesture made them look small and submissive before their leaders. Notice we don't genuflect before the Pope, or any bishop, for we are submissive to Christ alone.

15. St Augustine says, "*When people bend the knee or stretch out their hands, or even bow themselves down in prayer, they are using their bodies to show their inner spirit of prayer. He does not need those signs, but we need them, because they help us pray more humbly*". On the Trinity, 7.

16. Chadwick, Owen, 1995, *A History of Christianity*, St Martin's Press, New York, NY, 45-47

17. The Church has condemned any form of Santeria or worship of saints. We don't worship saints, instead we venerate them, and we ask them to intercede for us before Jesus Christ, our only Mediator. "*For after they have been received into their heavenly home and are present to the Lord, through him and with him and in him, they do not cease to intercede with the Father for us.*" Vatican II, Dogmatic Constitution on the Church, 49.

18. Gallwey P., 1902, The Watches Of The Sacred Passion With Before And After, Art And Book Company, London, UK, Vol. 1, 764

19. Cf. *Catholic Customs & Traditions*, 80

20. Cf. *Catholic Customs & Traditions*, 191 -195
21. "*He anointed you with oil upon your forehead in baptism, for the seal that you have of God; so that you may be made the engraving of the signet, the sanctuary of God*". St Justin the Martyr, *Mystagogical Lecture*, 4
22. Both Jews and Romans of the first centuries kept their oils, water and wines in containers called Ampullae. If they held wine, they were sealed with clay. If they contained oil, then a cloth was placed over them, or some aromatic herbs to keep it sweet. How Christians Said The First Mass, 101.
23. Optatus of Milevis, Against The Donatists, Book 6
24. The Catholic Encyclopedia Online, search word: Sanctuary
25. Newton Richard, 1923, *The Jewish Tabernacle And Its Furniture In Their Typical Teachings*, Biblo Bazaar, New York, NY, 362-364
26. "*Altare est Christus*", the Altar is Christ, a 600 AD saying found in Papal Mass document, Ordo Romanus I, translated in Andrieu Michael, *Les Ordines Romani*, Vol 2 No. 67.
27. St Ambrose, Letter 22:13
28. Optatus of Milevis, Against the Donatists, Book 6
29. The Catholic Encyclopedia Online, search word: Altar
30. *Catechism of the Catholic Church*, Nos. 1182 & 1383
31. Cf. *Catholic Customs & Traditions*, 113.
32. Pope St. Zephyrinus in 198 AD celebrated his Mass over the relics of martyr saints.
33. The night Jesus celebrated His Last Supper, in Jerusalem he said Mass over the relics of Kings and Prophets of God who had been buried all over the city hills. Later in Rome, Christians began to place relics of their saints in square altar stones. The Chalice and the Paten were then placed over the altar stone for the Eucharistic Consecration. Cf. How Christ Said The First Mass, 130.
34. "*The practice of the deposition of relics of Saints, even those not Martyrs, under the altar to be dedicated is fittingly retained. However, care should be taken to ensure the authenticity of such relics.*" GIRM, 302
35. Every day and every hour the Church constantly prays Mass to glorify God, "*For from the rising of the sun, even to its setting, in every place, incense is going to be offer to My Name and a sacrifice offering that is pure*". Malachi 1:11.
36. Tobin Greg, 2005, *Holy Father Pope Benedict XVI Pontiff For A New Era*, Sterling Publishing, New York, NY, 8-9
37. St. Benedict is the founder of monasticism in Europe during the 6th Century AD. As many monks were ordained priests, the need for Altars increased.

38. While I was in seminary in Rome from 1990 to 1998, many times I was the altar server at a private Mass. While the community below participated in the main Mass, upstairs, priests celebrated their own private Masses in 10 different side altars dedicated to the Mother of God or to a saint. These altars were attached to the wall and decorated with mosaics. We prayed softly in Latin.

39. Fushek, Dale & Doods Bill, 2002, *Your One Stop Guide to the Mass*, Servant Publications, Ann Arbor, MI, 40-42

40. The 4 types of candles can be subdivided in their use into two groups, Vigil, or Votive. Vigil, meaning to await, because they accompany us in prayer as we await the coming of the Lord. Votive, means vow, because it accompanies with a prayer asking for a favor in return for some sort of promise or vow.

41. Saints are not gods or semi-gods, they don't have any unusual powers. What they do have is a close friendship with the Blessed Trinity and immense concern for our salvation (Mark 9:4). We also know that they listen to our petitions since they are alive, which in turn they present before God (Luke 16:19). Cf. *Catholic Customs & Traditions*, 187-188

42. Many People think Altar candles originated at Masses prayed in the Catacombs. However, they originated in the Jewish feast of Seder or Passover, when the meal was celebrated with bees wax candles. These candles were blessed with special prayers.

43. In the Jewish home, before the Passover Meal started, the women lit 6 candles; to each lamp they held out their hands and prayed for the repose of the souls of their dead. The Jews during the time of Christ, believed that while the candles of Sabbath and feasts like the Passover burned, God allowed the souls of the dead to cool themselves in cold water, remaining there while the candles burned. The ancient Egyptians also believed the soul needed to go through seven gates of purification before its final rest. Zanolini Antonio, 1923, *Disputationes Ad Sacram Scripturam Spectantis de Festis et Sectis Judeorum*, n4.

44. The Paschal Candle has its origins in the Jewish Temple, where the seven branch candelabra inside the Holy of Holies was lit only by a priest, but where only six candles were lighted, the center one awaited the coming of the Messiah.

45. The Seder Meal, or Passover, was a family event, and each member had a role; children were to ask questions such as "*Why is this night important?*" while the women of the house were the only ones allowed to light the Seder Candle lights. The night that Jesus celebrated his last Seder Meal, he most likely had some of the women that accompanied him light the candles. Meagher,

James L., 1906, *How Christ Said The First Mass*, Christian Press Association Publishing Company, New York, NY, 343

46. *Catechism of the Catholic Church*, Nos. 1243 & 2466
47. The Catholic Encyclopedia Online, search word: Sacristy
48. Cf. *Architecture Of The Western World*
49. The Encyclopedia Britanica Online, search word: Sacristy
50. *The Catechism of the Catholic Church*, Nos. 1569, 1570
51. *The Catechism of the Catholic Church*, Nos. 1537, 1538
52. The Pope is the successor of the Apostle Peter, the first servant of unity. His brother Bishops are the successors of the other Apostles. Cf. *Holy Father Pope Benedict XVI Pontiff For A New Era*, Introduction, xii
53. Cf. *A History of Christianity*, 23
54. St. Irenaeus the Bishop of Lyons from 180 to 200 AD wrote regarding the primacy of the Bishop of Rome over the other bishops, in order to preserve the traditions given by the Lord. "*By pointing out here the successions of the bishops of the greatest and most ancient Church known to all. Founded and organized at Rome by two most glorious Apostles. Peter and Paul, that Church which has the tradition and the faith which comes down to us after having been announced to men by the Apostles. For with this Church, all the churches must agree it is in her that the faithful everywhere have maintained the Apostolic tradition*". Quoted by San Juan Catholic Seminars, 1993, *Beginning Apologetics How to Explain and Defend the Catholic Faith*, Farmington, NM, 17 note 15
55. *The Catechism of the Catholic Church*, Nos. 1140, 1143
56. Cf. *How Christ Said The First Mass*, 308-309
57. *The Catechism of the Catholic Church*, Nos. 873, 791
58. During Jesus' time, the High Priest wore a Turban or Miter which he removed at the moment of the daily sacrifice. When Jewish men celebrated the Passover Meal, they also removed their head-coverings. This is the reason why Bishops remove their Miter and Solideo during the Liturgy of the Eucharist.
59. The Catholic Encyclopedia Online, search word: Miter
60. Cf. *The Middle Sea A History Of The Mediterranean*, 32-33
61. The Catholic Encyclopedia Online, search word: Solideo
62. *The Catechism of the Catholic Church*, No. 2639
63. The Amice was originally used as a hood, then it was mandated to cover the priest's street clothes. Stravinskas Peter, 2000, *The Bible and the Mass*, Newman House, Mount Pocono, PA, 116
64. *The Catechism of the Catholic Church*, Nos. 1142, 1580
65. Cf. *A History of Christianity*, 34
66. Cf. *Sursum Corda This is the Mass*, 137

67. Every Archbishop wears over his chasuble a stole called the Pallium. This symbolizes his authority over an ecclesiastical province and his union with the Pope from whom he receives this garment.
68. St. Ireneus, Against Heresies, 3,3,3
69. Cf. *A History of Christianity,* 93
70. *The Catechism of the Catholic Church,* Nos. 77, 873
71. *The Catechism of the Catholic Church,* No. 2730
72. It is believed that Jesus, at the Last Supper, wore an ornamented mantle called in Hebrew *Imatia.* This was the garment used by prophets and Kings. His *Imatia* was the vestment the soldiers divided among themselves before His Crucifixion. The *Imatia* resembles the Roman *Chasuble,* now used by priests. Cf. *How Christ Said The First Mass 300-303.*
73. *The Catechism of the Catholic Church,* Nos. 875, 876, 1548, 2347
74. Cf. *Catholic Customs & Traditions: A Popular Guide,* 191
75. *"As to the deacons, let one of them attend upon the oblation of the Eucharist, another stand outside at the door, minding those who enter."* Didascalia, c.250 AD
76. For the Jews and second century Christians, a depiction of Jesus was impossible. The Bible said not to make any images of God, for God is impossible to visualize. In 403 AD, Bishop Epiphanius saw a picture of Christ woven into a curtain at a church in Palestine, and pulled it down. By 749 AD, John of Damascus, the last of the Church Fathers, held that by becoming a man, God made it possible to paint a portrait of that man, and God blesses the painter's art. If God can be upon an icon so can those men and women called Saints, who owe their greatness to Christ.
77. Icons were portraits of Saints or the Blessed Virgin Mary or Jesus. These portraits were more than artistic ornaments. In Constantinople, during the 6th century, icons became like relics of saints. The artist who painted the portrait of the saint, prayed while painting it. This signified that the soul of the saint was being imprinted in the icon. People began to use icons on their homes to protect them from illnesses, they were considered miraculous and votive candles were lighted to venerate them. There were stories of icons, which had been painted by no human artist. In Bologna Italy at the Shrine of Our Lady of St Luke, they preserve an icon of the Blessed Mother painted by St Luke. Cf. A History of Christianity, 115.
78. 1 Timothy 3:2
79. Tansey G. Richard and De La Croix Horst, 1986, Art Throgh The Ages Ancient, Medieval, And Non-European Art, HBJ, San Diego, CA, 227-230

80. The Church transformed its meaning to signify we are a pilgrim people on a journey to eternal life. Lumen Gentium, 1964, The Constitution on the Church, Second Vatican Council, Vatican City, Chapter 7.

81. The procession moves in slow progress towards the Altar, where God awaits His people. Jesus is not just our goal to get to, symbolized by the Altar, but He comes among us, symbolized by the Crucifix and in the person of the Priest. Stravinskas Peter, 2000, *The Bible and the Mass*, Newman House, Mount Pocono, PA, 14,15.

82. The Bishop's Staff is the symbol of the authority given to him by Christ. The shepherd's Staff is adorned with precious metals. When the server holds the Bishop's Staff, he does so turning the front to the side, for only the bishop can hold it frontwards. The bishop's Staff was first used in Constantinople. By 700 AD, the Spanish Bishops were using them as they processed into Church. By the year 1000 AD, Pope Sylvester II gave a Staff to all Bishops he created. Cf. A History of Christianity, 97.

83. When Emperor Constantine legalized Christianity in 313 AD, at the Edict of Milan, he conferred upon Bishops the same signs of honor given to public officials; including escorts carrying lights and incense during the processions.

84. *The Catechism of the Catholic Church*, Nos. 769, 1156, 1348

85. Quoted in the GIRM, 39

86. What a privilege it was for the Christians of the first centuries to have met the first disciples of Christ and received from them their Baptism. They had a new life through Baptism, and they came to Mass as one community to sing with joy. "Singing comes out of happiness, and if you look closer, out of love. To one who knows how to appreciate the 'new life' also knows how to sing a 'new song'". St Augustine, Sermon 34.1.

87. *The Catechism of the Catholic Church*, Nos. 1156, 1157, 1158

88. *The Catechism of the Catholic Church*, No. 1182

89. The Lectures of St. Cyril of Jerusalem to the Newly Baptized, *On the Sacred Liturgy And Communion*, Lecture V, 3

90. To 'Redeem' comes from the Latin 'Re-Emere' meaning to buy back. The Apostle Paul says we were purchased at a high price, by Jesus' violent death and blood. This is singularly different from being saved, for salvation depends mostly on God and partly on us by not making any obstacles to His Grace in our lives. This is hugely different from the Protestant view that we are saved. Cf. 76.2 "Keep the door of your heart shut, and frequently defend your forehead with the seal of the cross, lest the exterminator (the devil) find some unguarded spot in you". St. Jerome, Letter 130:9.

91. This gesture demonstrates that we Catholics believe in three persons in one God, the Trinity. Pope John XXII in 1334 declared the Sunday after Pentecost as Trinity Sunday. Cf. *Catholic Customs & Traditions: A Popular Guide*, 104-105

92. Christians of the 4th Century also added the acclamation, "Glory be to the Father, and to the Son, and to the Holy Ghost" and, while bowing, they responded, "As it was in the beginning, is now and ever shall be, world without end, Amen".

93. *"The two lower fingers of the right hand were bent slightly together to confess belief that Jesus is both Divine and Human. The upper three fingers remained open though, to confess Belief in the Father, Son and Holy Spirit, Three Persons in One God".* Theodoret, iv. Or. Vi. De Prov

94. *Sursum Corda This is the Mass, 13*

95. *The Catechism of the Catholic Church*, Nos. 1235, 2157, 2158

96. *"Of what use is it to make the Sign of the Cross upon your body if the Sign of the Cross is not upon your heart? God does not want us to simply make pictures of His signs, but to act upon them".* St. Augustine, St. Augustine, Commentary On Psalm 50:1

97. In 452 AD, Attila and his barbarian Huns destroyed Milan and headed towards Rome. Pope St Leo I, upon hearing the news, travelled for several days from Rome to Verona to meet face to face with the King of the Huns. There, after praying, he convinced his opponent to advance no further. When Pope Leo returned to Rome he wrote, "The Sign of the Cross makes all who have been regenerated in Christ kings, but the unction of the Holy Spirit consecrates priests". T.I. Sermon 4. In Natal. Ordin. C.I.

98. *The Catechism of the Catholic Church*, No. 1325

99. Every priest in a diocese prays the Mass representing his Bishop. For this reason during Easter Sunday, the greeting, "*The Lord be with you*" is reserved for the Bishop.

100. St. Augustine, Letter 214 to Valentinus

101. "Every legitimate celebration of the Eucharist is directed by the Bishop, either in person or through a priest who are his helpers". GIRM, 92 and Sacrosanctum Concilium, 1964, The Constitution on the Sacred Liturgy, Second Vatican Council, Vatican City, No.42.

102. Philemon 1:25

103. St. Hippolytus of Rome, 1892, The Apostolic Tradition, Translated by Burton Scott Easton and Gregory Dix, Edinburgh edition of the Fathers. Found in the Christians Classics Ethereal Library www.ccel.org

104. The Didache, 1884 translation of Isaac H. Hall and John T. Napier, Chapter 14,

105. The early Church understood that Baptism washed all sins away, but did not stop them from sinning. The need for constant purification through the Sacraments of Reconciliation was needed. Therefore, before joining in the Sacrifice of Jesus in the Mass, each Christian prayed, "*I Confess...*" only then could they join in saying "*We Believe...*" Cf. The Catechism of the Catholic Church, No. 1140.

106. GIRM, 51

107. The striking of the breast, for the Jews of the first centuries, was a sign for mourning. Dubruiel, Michael, 2002-2007, *The How-to Book of the Mass: Everything You Need to Know But No One Ever Taught You*, Our Sunday Visitor, Huntington, IN, 63.

108. Wegman Herman, 1967, *Christian Worship In The East And West, A Study Guide To Liturgical History*, Pueblo Publishing, New York, NY, 239-295

109. *The Catechism of the Catholic Church*, No. 1385

110. In its original meaning, the "Kyrie Eleison" is not begging God for mercy but rather praising Jesus for his ardent love for us. "His great love is without end... His mercy endures for ever". Psalm 118:1.

111. Cf. The Apostolic Constitutions, No. 161

112. There were many calamities during the centuries that followed the first millennium; plagues, the atrocities during the Crusades, barbarian invasions, clergy scandals, Popes that were corrupted; all led to focusing on the sinfulness of the people. Thus, the Kyrie took a penitential nature. Cf. *Sursum Corda This is the Mass*, 21.

113. GIRM, 51

114. The Catholic Encyclopedia Online, search word: Holy Water

115. Every Sunday is considered a mini Easter. And because this water is holy, we don't need words to purify ourselves, only our intention and the sprinkling by the Bishop.

116. *The Catechism of the Catholic Church*, Nos. 18, 45, 441, 514, 2639

117. Cf. The Apostolic Constitutions, 179 – 8:13, 10:17

118. 83.3 Cf. *Sursum Corda This is the Mass,* 23

119. *The Catechism of the Catholic Church*, Nos. 1154, 1184 and GIRM, 309

120. McBride Alfred, O Praem, 2006, *A Short History of the Mass*, St. Anthony Messenger Press, Cincinnati, OH, 26-28, 91-92

121. "*Let the reader stand upon a high place, Let him read the books of Moses, of Joshua the son of Nun, of the Judges, and of the Kings... and besides these, the books of the sixteen prophets*". The Apostolic Constitutions, 2:57

122. "*Let young people sit by themselves, if there is space for them; if not, let them stand. Let those who are already stricken in years*

sit in order. Children should stand aside, or let their fathers and mothers take them and remain standing with them. Et the younger women also sit by themselves, if there is space for them; but if there is not, let them stand behind the women. Let those women who are married with children be placed by themselves, but let the widows and older women sit by themselves... if a poor man or woman comes to you, especially if they are old, and there is no room, the deacon shall find a place for them, O bishop, even if you yourself must sit on the ground. You must not make distinctions between persons, if you want your service to please God'. Didascalia Apostolorum, c.250 AD

123. Cf. *Architecture Of The Western World,* 110-113

124. *The Catechism of the Catholic Church,* No. 1003

125. Cf. *A History of Christianity,* 47-51

126. Cf. *A Short History of the Mass,* 47

127. *The Catechism of the Catholic Church,* Nos. 1093, 1096, 1154

128. Cf. *Christian Worship In The East And West, A Study Guide To Liturgical History,* 96-97

129. St. Jerome, Commentariorum in Isaiam libri 18, prol.: Pl 24,17B

130. Cf. *The How-to Book of the Mass: Everything You Need to Know But No One Ever Taught You,* 106-107

131. Foley Edward, 2011, *A Commentary On The Order Of The Mass Of The Roman Missal,* A Pueblo Book Published by Liturgical Press, Collegeville, MN, 68

132. *The Catechism of the Catholic Church,* Nos. 128,129, 140, 2585, 2586, 2587

133. Quoted in the GIRM, 39

134. St Augustine, On Psalm 18:2

135. Moore Gerard, 2004, *Why The Mass Matters A Guide To Praying The Mass,* Pauline Books & Media, Boston, MA, 28-29

136. The Catholic Encyclopedia Online, search words: Gregorian Chant.

137. *The Catechism of the Catholic Church,* Nos. 785, 849, 2589

138. Attributed to St Augustine, Cf. Sermon 362:29; Exposition on Psalm 148

139. Quoted in *Sursum Corda This is the Mass,* 33. But most likely the authentic quote is, " "Our entire activity will be 'Amen' and 'Alleluia'". St. Augustine, Sermon 362,29 (PL 38:1224).

140. Most likely was Pope Gregory I, 590-604 AD, who allowed the Alleluia to be part of every Sunday Mass, except during Lent. Cf. Fushek, Dale & Doods Bill, 2002, *Your One Stop Guide to the Mass,* Servant Publications, Ann Arbor, MI, 68-69.

141. St. Benedict, Rule for Monasteries, 19

142. We stand up and welcome the Gospel proclamation with the same honor that we welcome the Eucharistic Lord. We stand firm, as the Book of Gospels might be escorted with incense and candles, just like a Roman Senator would have been, in the first centuries. We also stand because the Bible says that is the posture of those who await the return of Jesus. Cf. If Your Mind Wanders at Mass, 69-71.

143. Some Gospels might have claimed to be from Jesus' Wife. On September 18, 2012, an article in the New York Times describes the discovery of a fragment from a lost Gospel from Apostolic times, containing this quote, "Jesus said to them, 'My wife...'". This could be an authentic discovery; however, it only shows that the many opinions from the early Christians, in the end were submitted to scrutiny by the successors of the Apostles, in order to preserve the integrity of the teachings of Christ. Also, see A History of Christianity, 47-48. Also, see the Catholic Encyclopedia Online search word: Gospel.

144. GIRM, 133

145. Quoted by Guardini Romano, 1993, *Meditations Before Mass*, Sofia Institute Press, Manchester, NH, 99

146. *The Catechism of the Catholic Church*, Nos. 53, 103, 457, 1270

147. GIRM, 134

148. St Justin Martyr, op cit, 67

149. *The Catechism of the Catholic Church*, Nos. 108, 787, 796, 862, 1163, 1349

150. A creed is like having a map of a city, where the streets and the roads are defined. In the same way, the Creed helps us know what we believe about our Faith. One day in Heaven, we won't need a Creed any longer, for we shall know God.

151. St Hippolytus of Rome, *The Apostolic Tradition*, 21

152. Davis Leo Donald, 1983, *The First Seven Ecumenical Councils (325-787) Their History and Theology*, A Michael Glazier Book, The Liturgical Press, Collegeville, MN, 33-69

153. Van Dorsen Charles, 1991, *A History of Knowledge Past, Present, and Future, The pivotal events, people, and achievements of world history*, Ballantine Books, New York, NY, 91-95

154. *The Catechism of the Catholic Church*, Nos. 185, 186, 187, 188

155. Cf. *Christian Worship In The East And West, A Study Guide To Liturgical History*, 22, 72, 184

156. A sample for the Prayers of the Faithful from the 5th Century: "*Let us all, the faithful beseech God fervently: for the peace and tranquility of the world, and the holy churches... for those who are afflicted by sickness, for those who are traveling by land and sea... for those condemned to the mines, to exile, to prison, and*

fetters for the sake of the Name of the Lord...for every departed Christian soul..." The Apostolic Constitutions, vii, 10, 1-22

157. *The Catechism of the Catholic Church*, Nos. 1349, 1366
158. *The Catechism of the Catholic Church*, Nos. 1351, 2043.2
159. St Justin the Martyr, *1 Apology*, 67
160. Cf. *The How-to Book of the Mass: Everything You Need to Know But No One Ever Taught You*, 159
161. *The Catechism of the Catholic Church*, Nos. 1350, 1383, 1397
162. *Sursum Corda This is the Mass*, 51
163. GIRM 73, 74
164. Rev. Brian Bashista, Conference given on Vocations at the Diocese of Lexington, KY, August, 2009
165. Cf. *A History of Christianity*, 22
166. *Catholic Customs & Traditions: A Popular Guide*, 185
167. *The Catechism of the Catholic Church*, No. 1186
168. This linen is folded in 9 parts on which the chalice and paten rest during the Sacrifice. Cf. *How Christ Said The First Mass*, 374.
169. *The Catechism of the Catholic Church*, No. 1182
170. Cf. *Why The Mass Matters A Guide To Praying The Mass*, 47-52.
171. According to the Liber Pontificalis c.XVI De Manjarres Jose D, 1887, *Nociones de Arqueologia Cristiana Para Uso de los Seminarios Conciliares, Guia de Parrocos Y Juntas de Obra Y Fabricas De Las Iglesias*, Imprenta del Herredero de D. Pablo Riera, Barcelona, Espana. 149
172. *The Catechism of the Catholic Church*, No. 1379
173. *The Catechism of the Catholic Church*, Nos. 1334, 1339, 1340, 1367
174. Wood has always been a commodity in Palestine. For many centuries before the birth of Christ, Jews baked their unleavened bread in ovens. Many times these were heated by dried dung. The unleavened bread, called Matzah, reminded them of the time when God delivered them from slavery in Egypt. The Jews had to omit the yeast from the Matzah, since there was not time to prepare for the journey. The bread was then used for the Passover meal; broken and shared with all, by the head of the household. Cf. *How Christ Said The First Mass*, 89-91.
175. The Jews expelled Christians from all their synagogues in 100 AD. Some Christians thought they should do the opposite of what Jews had done, in order to distance themselves from any Jewish traditions. Thus, during the Seder Meal, they had leavened bread instead. This gave rise to a new heresy called Ebionite, condemned by the Church in 140 AD.
176. St John Chrysostom, *Sermon on the Gospel of St Matthew*
177. GIRM 142

178. Cf. *The Bible and the Mass*, 120
179. The ritual for the Seder Meal, or Passover, calls for having several napkins on the table; during the meal, these were used to cover the cups of wine and the dishes containing the Matzah bread and bitter herbs. Jesus, at his Last Supper, also used these napkins to cover the cup containing His Blood and the dish containing His Body.
180. Cf. *The Bible and the Mass,* 119
181. *The Catechism of the Catholic Church*, No. 1379
182. Around the year 1400 BC, Moses and the Hebrews were freed from the slavery of Egypt by God. For the next 40 years, they wandered in the desert on their way to the Promised Land. Every day during these 40 years, God fed his people with "Manna", a bread that came down in the morning. Manna in Hebrew means, "What is this?" The left over Manna was kept inside the Jewish Tabernacle, contained in a ciborium dish that today reminds us of the Eucharistic Bread kept in our Tabernacles throughout the world. See How Christ Said The First Mass, 20-21.
183. Cf. *Sursum Corda This is the Mass,* 57
184. The Eucharist without the Wine is not the Eucharist, because it fails to reproduce what Jesus did at the Last Supper, and we would be disobeying his command, "Do this... in memory of me". Cf. *The Bible and the Mass*, 54
185. *The Catechism of the Catholic Church*, No. 1350
186. "*The deacons shall hold the cups, and stand with reverence and dignity; first the one who holds the water, next the milk, then the wine. The recipients shall taste 3 times from each. He who gives the cup shall say: 'In God the Father Almighty.' And the recipient shall say: 'Amen.' Then 'In the Lord Jesus Christ.' And he shall say: 'Amen.' Then 'In the Holy Ghost and holy Church. And he shall say 'Amen' And when these things are completed, let each hasten to do good and please God and live right* ". St Hippolytus of Rome, *The Apostolic Tradition*, Translation by Burton Scott Easton (1934) and Gregory Dix (1937)
187. The Priest uses the same prayer said by Azariah, one of the 3 young men in the fiery furnace mentioned in the Book of Daniel 3:39. This prayer was officially made part of the Preparation of the Gifts in 1570 when Pope St Pius V codified the Roman Missal.
188. *The Catechism of the Catholic Church*, Nos. 1186, 1333, 1350
189. Christians from the first three centuries did not use Incense for Mass because it was not part of the ritual of Jesus at the Last Supper. Also, for these Jewish converts, Incense was associated with the Incense in the Temple of Jerusalem, or with the Incense used by pagan Romans and Greeks, when worshiping their gods.

After the Church accepted incense for the Mass, the community prayed as the Minister Incensed them and the Gifts. "Let our sacrifice be spotless and pleasing to God".

190. *The Catechism of the Catholic Church*, No. 1383
191. Guardini Romano, 1956, *Sacred Signs*, Pio Decimo Press, St Louis, MO, 15-18
192. This gesture is a symbol for Jesus washing the feet of Peter at the Last Supper. Peter didn't want to, but Jesus rebuked him, and Peter said, "Not only wash my feet but also my hands and my face". This is a symbol of purification from the early Mass of c29 AD, and cannot be omitted.
193. St Cyril of Jerusalem, *Mystagogical Lecture,* 5
194. GIRM, 76, 145
195. The Priest is aware that our sacrifice offered to God can be acceptable or not. Cain, son of Adam, offered a sacrifice not pleasing to God. (Genesis 4:5) Other times, there were Jewish Priests that offered a sacrifice to God but the Bible says, "I have no pleasure in you says the Lord of Hosts, and I will not accept an offering from your hand". (Malachi 1:10)
196. Cf. *Sursum Corda This is the Mass*, 65
197. GIRM, 146
198. *The Catechism of the Catholic Church*, Nos. 1128, 1547, 1552
199. *The Catechism of the Catholic Church*, Nos. 823, 829
200. St. Hippolytus, Apostolic Tradition, 36 Anaphora
201. St Cyril of Jerusalem, *The Catechetical Lectures*, 8, 48e
202. "*You are attended by thousands upon thousands and myriads upon myriads of Angels and Archangels, of Thrones and Dominations, of Principalities and Powers. Beside You stand the two August Seraphim with six wings, two to cover their face, two to cover their feet, two with which to fly. They sing your holiness. With theirs, accept also our acclamation of Your Holiness, Holy, Holy, Holy is the Lord Sabaoth! Heaven and earth are filled with Your Glory. The heaven is filled, the earth is filled with Your wonderful glory!".* Euchology, *Prayer of the Anaphora*, 13
203. GIRM, 79
204. Praying 'Holy, Holy, Holy, Lord...' is like giving God a standing ovation for all He has done for us.
205. Council of Nicaea I, Cannon 18 Also see, Davis Leo Donald, 1983, *The First Seven Ecumenical Councils (325-787) Their History and Theology*, A Michael Glazier Book, The Liturgical Press, Collegeville, MN, 67-68
206. Cf. *The How-to Book of the Mass: Everything You Need to Know But No One Ever Taught You,* 172
207. *The Catechism of the Catholic Church*, No. 563

208. *The Catechism of the Catholic Church*, Nos. 611, 1364, 1366, 1378
209. Cf. *The Bible and the Mass*, 58-78
210. St Cyril of Jerusalem, *Mystagogical Lecture, 4*
211. *The Catechism of the Catholic Church*, No. 1672
212. The use of bells, for the early Christian community, was not permitted, as these were used in Rome and Egypt for pagan events. Bells were invented in China. These were used in pagan temples for casting spells, or keeping evil spirits away. The Romans used bells during the cult of their gods Mithras and Baccus; these were rung violently to urge worshipers to ecstasy. When pagans became Catholic, they first used their bells during storms to protect themselves from lighting or fires.
213. Bells helped people know the key moments when the priest lifted the Body and Blood of Christ at the Altar. At this time, the priest prayed in a low voice in Latin, also, in some large churches, the Choir area stood between the congregation and the Sanctuary, making it difficult for people to see and hear the Priest.
214. *The Catechism of the Catholic Church*, Nos. 1146, 1338, 1353, 1356, 1362, 1367
215. St Cyril of Jerusalem, *Mystagogical Lecture, 5*
216. In the year 29 AD, all Jewish families celebrated the Seder Meal, or Passover. The head of the Jewish household took the Matzah bread, and, after blessing it, elevated it and presented it to his family by moving his hands forward towards the west, then back, to the east, then back, to the south, back, and north and back. After this, he broke the bread and kept one piece hidden under the napkin, to represent the Manna from heaven that was to come when they least expected it. Then, he shared the rest of the blessed bread with his family. Jesus did the same with his disciples, but alternatively he gave them His Own Flesh instead of Matzah, the real bread from Heaven. This movement was known as the Terumah. The High Priest did the same at the temple while presenting the lamb for the sacrifice. Several priests held the animal from the bottom and lifted it up before the Terumah. Cf. *Disputationes Ad Sacram Scripturam Spectantis de Festis et Sectis Judaeorum, c.iv* and *How Christ Said The First Mass*, 188, 413-415
217. *The Catechism of the Catholic Church*, No. 1370
218. St Augustine, *The City Of God*, Book 9, 13:66 online version.
219. GIRM 79h
220. St Agustine, *Sermons*
221. *The Catechism of the Catholic Church*, Nos. 1266, 2670, 2856.
222. GIRM 81.

223. Praying 54 Our Fathers every day became the new tradition for the converts to Christianity of the first two centuries as they replaced the Jewish ritual of praying 54 Benedictions known as the "*Shemoneh Esreh*". (See note 294) By 311 AD, St Anthony of Egypt, moved to the desert to become the first monk to pray in solitude. There, he prayed 54 Our Fathers, and 150 psalms per day. Soon, many others joined him in monastic life. Bishop St Basil of Caeserea, in 370 AD, encouraged all monks to pray without ceasing; (1 Thessalonians 5:17) thus, all monks who could not read the psalms, prayed 50 or 150 times the Our Father prayer instead. To make it easy to count prayers, they tied knots around a rope, which came to be known as the Chotki, or prayer rope. The Chotki became the predecessor of the Rosary beads. For more turn to page 88. From a conference at the Athenaeum Pontificium Regina Apostolorum, in Rome, March 1998.

224. St Cyprian of Carthage, *On The Lord's Prayer*, 18.

225. *The Catechism of the Catholic Church*, Nos. 1265, 2777, 2842, 2845.

226. Didache, Chapter 9.

227. St Cyril of Jerusalem, *Mystagogical Lecture*, 5.

228. *The Catechism of the Catholic Church*, Nos.1130, 2760, 2855.

229. *The Catechism of the Catholic Church*, No. 1345.

230. Pope Innocent I, Apostolic Letter Decentio Augubino.

231. The Church does not define peace as the absence of war. "*Peace cannot be attain on earth without safeguarding the goods of persons and peoples, and the assiduous practice of fraternity. Peace is the tranquility of order. Peace is the work of justice and the effect of charity*". Lumen Gentium, 1964, *The Constitution on the Catholic Church*, Second Vatican Council, Vatican City, 78:1-2.

232. GIRM, 82.

233. Over Mount Moriah, Salomon built a Temple for God, the Temple of Jerusalem. (2 Chronicles 3:1) Animal Sacrifices were offered daily on behalf of the people. Scharfstein Sol, 2008, *Torah, And Commentary: The Five Books Of Moses, Translation Rabbinic and Contemporary Commentary*, KTAV Publishing House, Jersey City, NJ. 78, Note 14.

234. GIRM, 83, 321.

235. *Pars Inferior Praecidi Debet* – S.R.C., 4 August 1663.

236. *The Catechism of the Catholic Church*, Nos. 1137, 1329, 1602, 1612.

237. *The Catechism of the Catholic Church*, Nos. 1385, 1386, 1387.

238. St Cyril of Jerusalem, *Mystagogical Lecture, 5.*

239. Cf. *Catholic Customs & Traditions: A Popular Guide*, 35, 78.

240. GIRM 160, 161.

241. St Cyril of Jerusalem, *Mystagogical Lecture, 5*.

242. The Lectionary of Bernward of Hildesheim (1022 AD).

243. Pope Gelasius I, in 480 AD, declared that the Baptized should receive Communion of Both the Body and Blood without abstaining from one or the other. "*They should either receive the Sacrament in its entirety or be kept from it altogether, since it is impossible to separate one and the same Mystery without severe sacrilege*". Cf. *Sursum Corda This is the Mass*, 117.

244. St Justin the Martyr, *First Apology, 65.*

245. St Cyril of Jerusalem, *Mystagogical Lecture, 5.*

246. St Augustine, Sermon No. 272, also quoted in *The Catechism of the Catholic Church*, No. 1396.

247. Interview with Card. Antonio Canizares Llovera, Vatican Prefect for the Office of Divine Worship, ACI Prensa, July 27, 2011 "*We recommend that the faithful receive communion on the tongue and while kneeling, this is simple, we recognize that we are in front of God Himself who comes to us.*"

248. In 379 AD, St Basil mentions in his writings the Pyx in a form of a dove. Cf. A Short History of the Mass, 48.

249. GIRM, 314 and *Eucharisticum Mysterium*, 52, GIRM, 315 also mentions that "*It is more appropriate as a sign that on an Altar on which Mass is celebrated there not be a tabernacle in which the Most Holy Eucharist is reserved (cf. Eucharisticum Mysterium 55) Consequently, it is preferable that the tabernacle be located according to the judgment of the diocesan Bishop: a) either in the sanctuary, apart from the altar of celebration, in a appropriate form and place, not excluding its being positioned on an old altar no longer used for the celebration (cf. no. 303); b) or even in some chapel suitable for the private adoration and prayer of the faithful and organically connected to the church and readily noticeable by the Christian faithful. (Code of Cannon Law 938, 2)* I have seen Cathedrals, like Christ the King in Lexington Kentucky USA, where the Tabernacle was placed in the center of the Sanctuary, a particularly prominent place but detached from the Altar, and this makes the Sacrifice of the Mass appropriate and dignified.

250. *The Catechism of the Catholic Church*, No. 2691.

251. *Catholic Customs & Traditions: A Popular Guide*, 188.

252. St Augustine, *Anti Pelagian Writings: On St Sixtus;* 1 Corinthians 4:16.

253. GIRM, 163.

254. St. Hippolytus, *Apostolic Tradition, 46.*

255. *The Catechism of the Catholic Church*, Nos. 1332, 1334, 1405.

256. GIRM, 167.
257. St Justin the Martyr, *First Apology, 65.*
258. Cf. A History of the Mass, 70-81.
259. Cantalamessa Rev. Raniero, *2nd Lenten Homily, Christ Offered Himself to God,* Vatican City, March 15, 2010, Zenit.org
260. Cf. *A History of Knowledge Past, Present, and Future, The pivotal events, people, and achievements of world history,* 91-95.
261. Philocallian Calendar of 354 AD.
262. For the Jews who became Christians during Jesus' time, it was common to consider water as blessed and miraculous. We learned in the Gospel (John 5:1) that outside the Jerusalem Temple sat a paralytic man who was in need of healing. He begged Jesus to heal him because he could not get in the pool when the miraculous waters moved. Cf. *The Apocryphal Gospel of the Hebrews.* 75:2 also the Didache Chapter 7 calls the water of Baptism *"Living Water".*
263. *"And then putting on the over-garment of pure white linen without spot or seam, he sat at the table'. The Apocryphal Gospel of the Hebrews.* 76:1.
264. *Cf. The Apocryphal Gospel of the Hebrews.* 76:8.
265. *Cf. The Apocryphal Gospel of the Hebrews.* 75:6.
266. According to the *Apocryphal Gospel of the Hebrews,* Jesus says that Celibacy is not for everyone but for those given this gift. Also, Jesus mentions that those from the community who have been given the gift of healing also have been asked to keep their seed inside and to abstain from sexual contact, so the Power of God would be working from within. "The power of healing comes from perfect chastity and faith". *Cf. The Apocryphal Gospel of the Hebrews.* 92:4
267. 'Kleros' meas to "Cast Lots". Acts 1:26 used the word Cleric in Greek, 'Kleros', when the 11 Apostles met in order to elect a new successor to replace Judas who betrayed Jesus. They didn't vote, rather they wrote the names of various people and drew a name while in prayer. The heritage was passed on to Matthias who was chosen to become a Bishop. From the very start, the Apostles were concerned to pass on the Mission entrusted to them by Jesus, to their successors.
268. According to one of the Apocryphal Gospels, one of the disciples asked Jesus, after the Resurrection, whether his Ministers should allow fancy garments when presiding over the community; He answered them that, for the moment, they should continue to wear the white linen spotless garment, but the day was coming when they were going to rejoice and wear beautiful garments. *Cf. The Apocryphal Gospel of the Hebrews.* 94.5.

269. Covenant means a Testament or Will. For the ancient Hebrew people, the Covenant was a sacred family bond, an agreement given by God between Him and His people. When God gave Moses the two tablets with the 10 Commandments, he asked him to build an Ark of the Covenant. This was a wooden chest carried by the Hebrews while wandering in the desert for 40 years. After this, Salomon placed it inside the Temple at Jerusalem.

270. Before Jesus' Resurrection, a place of burial was commonly known as the City of Death, in Greek, Necropolis. After His Resurrection, the new name became Cemetery, or the Dormitory in Greek 'Kemeterion'.

271. Durant Will, 1950, *Age of Faith*, Simon & Schuster, New York, NY, 856.

272. Count Guelfo Della Gherardesca mentioned these facts during my meeting with him at his office speaking of the history of Della Guerardesca and Medici banking family. Firenze, Italy, May 1996.

273. Norrington David, 1996, *To Preach or Not To Preach? The Church's Urgent Question*, Paternoster Press, Carlisle, UK, 23.

274. Some people think that a priest confines God to a piece of bread. In reality, it is God who decided to be truly present in a piece of bread. My grandmother used to say, if I broke a mirror in various pieces and I looked at it, my reflection would have been in every single piece of glass. The same happens in the Eucharist though it not only reflects God it becomes God the Son, even in a single particle, while He continues to be infinite. This is the mystery of our Faith.

275. The Martyrs of Abitina in North Africa died in 304 AD. They refuse to renounce their faith in Jesus in the Eucharist. They died saying, "We cannot live without the Eucharist" The Roman Martyrology remembers them on February 12 as their feast day.

276. In 2011, Archeologist Phillip DiBlasi from the University of Louisville KY, performed forensic studies on the bones of St Bonosa, a 24 year old from c207 AD, who died a martyr in Rome. Her bones showed that she used to kneel much. Louisville's *Courier-Journal*, September 23, 2012.

277. The Tree of Paradise represents the Garden of Eden where Adam and Eve lived. According to the Book of Genesis, the Serpent gave a fruit from the tree of Knowledge of Good and Evil to Adam to eat. As early as the 6th Century we hear of depictions of the Tree of Paradise displayed in Jewish synagogues in the form of mosaics. Several of these mosaics can be seen today at the Brooklyn Museum in New York. The 12th Century, troubadours were traveling singing poets who acted various stories, including

religious themes. Because they constantly traveled, they also carried local traditions and customs from one region to the next. On December 24, during the Byzantine feast of Adam and Eve, the troubadours acted the story of Adam and Eve, in which they displayed the Tree of Paradise on stage. By the 17th Century, this tree was commonly known as the Christmas tree.

278. Before 313 AD, Christians were a home-centered church. In many places, they were not permitted to erect church buildings. However, In Siria, archeologist found the house of Dura-Europos as a private home in which Christians in 235 AD, gathered for Mass. These homes though they belonged to an individual family they were considered holy, special, and sacred. The term 'Church' in Greek is 'Ekklesia', and when St Paul uses this word in the Bible it means, 'Congregation' instead of a building. When he wants to say a church as a building he uses the terms, 'Oikos tou Theou' translated as 'The Home of God'. *"The Home of God [Oikos tou Theou] which is the Church [Ekklesia] of the living God"* (1 Timothy 3:15). See Viola Frank, and Barna George, 2008, *Pagan Christianity*, Tyndale House Publishers, Carol Stream, IL, 10-25.

279. Cf. *How Christ Said The First Mass*, 70-71.

280. The '*Cohanim Blessing*' gesture is similar to the popular "Vulcan salute". The hands are raised forward with the fingers parted between the middle and the ring finger. When both hands come together, their fingers form a triangle symbol, which symbolized the Providence of God. When the Jewish high priest blessed those in the Temple, the Jews covered their heads in reverence and were not allowed to see the Cohanim gesture from the priest's hands.

281. Since the year 800 AD, people had stopped receiving the Blood of Christ at Communion since they felt unworthy. At this time, the Church saw the need to interrupt the procession from families at the Offertory and instead the Altar Servers brought the Offertory from the Credence Table to the Altar. Cf. page 72

282. Saturnalia was an ancient Roman festivity from the year 217 BC. For seven, days, beginning on every December 17, Romans celebrated a time of liberation and freedom from mortality, and morality, or as Seneca put it, "*a time to throw off the toga*". People sacrificed animals at the temple of Saturn at the foot of the Capitoline Hill, in the west end of the Forum Romanum. No public business was allowed. Saturn was considered the god of abundance, and for the Romans there was no better way to invite all future abundance into their lives than to celebrate in abundance. On December 23, all Romans gave gifts to each other calling this day the Sigillaria day. On this day, some people gave

each other small figurine statues, candles, pottery and some oddities such as "gag gifts" or practical jokes. During this festivity, the slaves had the freedom of speech. They could criticize their masters. Also, slave owners could free some of their slaves by granting them the Pilleolus' cap and allowing them to dine at the table with them. This festivity time was considered the happiest times in Rome since people sang jovially, drank lots of alcohol, ate and gambled much, and wore masks. All preparing for the birth of the new Sun God, the invincible Sun, "Sol Invictus" on December 25.

283. Church Council of Ephesus

284. Church Council of Constantinople

285. The Church organized the prayer of the Hail Mary in two parts. The first taken from the Gospel of Luke 1:28 when the Angel greets her, "*Hail, Mary, full of grace; the Lord is with thee.*" then from Luke 1:42 the Church added the words of Elizabeth when Mary visited her, "*Blessed art thou amongst women, and blessed is the fruit of thy womb*". The second part comes as a petition from the Church, "*Holy Mother, of God, pray for us sinners now and at the hour of our death, Amen*".

286. They are called Mysteries because we meditate on 15 various mysteries of the life of Jesus from His Mother's perspective. The first five are the Joyous Mysteries, for we meditate on the Annunciation by the Angel, The Visitation of Mary to her cousin Elizabeth, the Nativity, the Presentation of Jesus at the Temple as a baby, and the Finding of Jesus at the Temple, when he was 12 years old. The second are the Sorrowful Mysteries, for we meditate on Jesus' Agony at the Garden, the Scourging, the Crowning with Thorns, Carrying of the Cross and the Crucifixion. And last five are the Glorious Mysteries, for we contemplate our Lord's Resurrection, Ascension into Heaven, then the Coming of the Holy Spirit at Pentecost, then Mary's Assumption into Heaven, and the Coronation of Mary as Queen of Heaven. All these Mysteries were published in a book in 1489. In 2002 Pope John Paul II added a new Mystery called Luminous, so we could ponder on Jesus' Baptism at the Jordan river, the Wedding at Cana, the time when Jesus Proclaimed his Kingdom, the Transfiguration of Jesus before his disciples, and the Institution of the Eucharist at the Last Supper.

287. Cf. A History of Christianity, 135-142. The positive medical effects of praying the Rosary were documented in the British Medical Journal (2201; 323:1446-1449). Researcher, Dr. Luciano Bernardi, associate professor of internal medicine at the University of Pavia in Italy, and his team tested whether a

rhythmic chanting, in this case praying the Rosary, could have a favorable effect on the heart's rhythm. What they found was that praying the Rosary slowed the patient's hearts from 14 breaths a minute to 6. *"Breathing at a rate of 6 breaths per minute has favorable effects on cardiovascular and respiratory function"*. The researchers noted. Shaw Roxana, October 9, 2012, *Praying The Rosary Is As Good As Yoga For Your Health*, The Huffington Post Journal

288. *The Catechism of the Catholic Church*, No. 210. The Church does not describe Purgatory as a place, rather as a 'state' of purification.

289. The Roman Dictator Lucius Quinctius Cincinnatus in the Battle of Mons Algidus in 458 BC defeated the Aequi people. Their leaders became prisoners of war and in order to validate their defeat they had to submit by bowing down before the Dictator. This is one of the earliest accounts of bowing down in western history.

290. Please note that the book of Maccabees is an approved book of the Bible for us Catholics. Protestants, on the other hand, believe this book does not form part of the Bible, calling it an Apocryphal book. The term Apocryphal means, of doubtful authenticity. To learn more see Page 54 and Note # 292.

291. The word saint means set apart, not contaminated, perfect, full of God's grace. For the newly baptized of the first centuries they were aware of their greatness, for Scripture stated clearly that they were created in the image and likeness of God. (Genesis 1:27) Through baptism, this image was once again restored to its original beauty. Then it meant that, in their beings, they must already be perfect. The more they accepted this truth, the more they were able to express and manifest that perfection in their actions and interactions with the world affairs and one another. These saints fulfilled the Lord Jesus' words, *"For the Kingdom of God is within you"*, (Luke 17:21).

292. Around 90 AD, Rabbi Yochanan ben Zakkai, managed to escape Jerusalem inside a coffin before its destruction and received approval to rebuild a Jewish base in the city of Jamnia. There, he gathered other rabbis to establish the cannon for the Hebrew Bible. They wanted to make sure only Books written in Hebrew would be part of their Bible, rejecting all Greek Old Testament books called the Septuagint. For Hebrew was considered God's only language. Greek books like the Book of Maccabees were rejected. The Catholic Bishops, on the other hand, were open to accept the Books written in Greek.

293. St Cyril of Jerusalem, *Catechetical Lectures*, 28,23.

294. *Shemoneh Esreh* is a collection of 54 benedictions divided into 18 prayers recited three times a day in ancient synagogues. These prayers were divided according to their content in three groups: three blessings of praise to God, followed by twelve petitions, concluded by three thanksgiving prayers. An example of one of these prayers reads, "Blessed be Thou, O Lord, 'Adonai', our God and God of our fathers, God of Abraham, God of Isaac, God of Jacob, the great, the mighty, and the fearful God – God Most High – who bestowest goodly kindnesses, and art the Creator of all, and rememberest the love for the Fathers, and bringest a redeemer for their children's children for the sake of Thy name in love. King, Helper, Savior, and Shield, blessed be Thou, Shield of Abraham." Jewish Encyclopedia, online reference, Jewishencyclopedia.com

295. The third century catacomb of St Marcelinus and St Peter in Rome portrays depictions of Jonah inside a fish as a symbol for Christ. (Jonah 1:17).

296. Exorcism comes from the Greek word "Exorkismos" meaning Binding Oath. For Christians, it means the exercise of evicting demons from a person's body, mind and soul.

297. The reason there are six candles at Sunday Mass is because we imitate the Lord Jesus' first Mass. All Jewish families of the year 29 AD lit six candles at sundown at their homes during the celebration of Passover. Only in the Temple of Jerusalem, the Jewish high priest was allowed to light the solid gold, 100 pounds candelabra, which held seven lamps. Each of these lights symbolized the creation days and the awaiting of the coming of the Messiah. Cf. *How Christ Said The First Mass*, 24, 25, 343 - 345.

298. The paten was used by altar servers during Communion, by placing it under the chin of the communicant, to catch the Blessed Host if it should fall from the Minister's hands. Cf. *The Bible and the Mass*, 121.

299. Cf. *Nociones de Arqueologia Cristiana Para Uso de los Seminarios Conciliares, Guia de Parrocos Y Juntas de Obra Y Fabricas De Las Iglesias*, 209 – 210.

300. Cf. *Nociones de Arqueologia Cristiana*, 218

301. In some sarcophagi, within the catacombs or Rome, the Alpha and Omega symbols were at times preceded by Roman numbers, also symbols of realities. For example, the Roman numeral "X" for ten, symbolized Christ the perfect healer of the soul. The number forty or "XL" was the symbol for perfect virginity and martyrdom. The number 30 or "XXX" was for the perfect marriage in Christ. Some converts to Christianity from Judaism had knowledge of

numerology, the study of the mystical relation between numbers and events.

302. Pert Candace PhD, 1999, *Molecules of Emotion The Science Behind Mind-Body Medicine*, Simon & Schuster, New York, NY, 63

303. Sin is a violation of God's natural law and love, revealed to us primarily through Scripture, and the Teachings of the Church. Sin comes from a Greek word meaning missing the mark or target. My grandmother Adela explained sin to me. "You take some nails and a hammer, and you may fix things at home. However, you may also use them improperly. Let's say you start nailing the surface of the expensive coffee table made from Carpathian Elmwood. I am going to be disappointed, for you have ruined a beautiful table and gone against my wishes. I love you, I will forgive you, but you still have to remove those nails, and fix the wholes. The plush table is an image for your soul and the nails for sin. The gravity of sin depends on the nail's size and the degree of deliberate selfish intention in your heart." Any small nails on the fine table's surface would be called in Catholic terms, Venial sins. Large nails that have ruined the valuable table and rapport with grandma are called, Grave or Mortal sins, for it has deadly consequences for the soul. A person goes to confession to remove both Venial and Mortal sins. Purgatory then is for those who have died with un-repented Venial sins and still need to remove and fix the wholes on the table.

304. *The Catechism of the Catholic Church*, Nos. 1030-1032

BIBLIOGRAPHY

Archdiocese of Sydney, 2008, *Sursum Corda This is the Mass*, Sydney, Australia

Aquila James, 2000, *The Mass of the Early Christians*, Our Sunday Visitor, Huntington, IN

Arinze Francis Cardinal, 2006, *Celebrating the Holy Eucharist*, Ignatius Press, San Francisco, CA

Bashista Rev. Brian, August 2009, Conference given on vocations at the Diocese of Lexington, KY

Burkitt F.C, 1923, *The Early Syrian Lectionary System, 6th Century, The British Academy*, Oxford University Press, London

Britannica Encyclopedia, online reference, Britannica.com

Cantalamessa Raniero, O.F.M. March 15, 2010, 2nd Lenten Homily, *Christ Offered Himself to God*, Vatican City, Zenit.org

Catechism of the Catholic Church, Vatican website: Vatican.va

Chadwick Owen, 1995, *A History of Christianity*, St Martin's Press, New York, NY

Davis Leo Donald, 1983, *The First Seven Ecumenical Councils (325-787) Their History and Theology*, A Michael Glazier Book, The Liturgical Press, Collegeville, MN

Davies J.G., 1968, *The Secular Use of Church Buildings*, The Seabury Press, New York, NY

De Manjarres Jose D, 1887, *Nociones de Arqueologia Cristiana Para Uso de los Seminarios Conciliares, Guia de Parrocos Y Juntas de Obra Y Fabricas De Las Iglesias*, Imprenta del Herredero de D. Pablo Riera, Barcelona, Espana.

Dubruiel Michael, 2002-2007, *The How-to Book of the Mass: Everything You Need to Know But No One Ever Taught You*, Our Sunday Visitor, Huntington, IN

Dues Greg, 1992, *Catholic Customs & Traditions: A Popular Guide*, Twenty-third Publications, Mystic, CT

Durant Will, 1950, *Age of Faith*, Simon & Schuster, New York, NY

Early Church Fathers, Online Resources by Christian Classics Ethereal Library, ccel.org

Encyclopedia Britannica, Online

Foley Edward, 2011, *A Commentary On The Order Of The Mass Of The Roman Missal*, A Pueblo Book Published by Liturgical Press, Collegeville, MN

Fushek Dale & Doods Bill, 2002, *Your One Stop Guide to the Mass*, Servant Publications, Ann Arbor, MI

Gallwey P., 1902, *The Watches Of The Sacred Passion With Before And After,* Art And Book Company, London, UK, Vol. 1

General Instruction of the Roman Missal, GIRM, 2003, The Order of Mass

Guardini Romano, 1993, *Meditations Before Mass*, Sofia Institute Press, Manchester, NH

Guardini Romano, 1956, *Sacred Signs*, Pio Decimo Press, St Louis, MO

Howard Thomas, 1995, *If Your Mind Wanders at Mass*, Ignatius Press, San Francisco, CA

International Committee on English in the Liturgy, *The Order of Mass* 1, 2006 – 2008,1

Johnson Kevin Orlin, 1994, *Why Do Catholics Do That? A Guide to the Teachings and Practices of the Catholic Church*, Ballantine Books, New York, NY

Justin St. Martyr, Apologia I & II, online

Jewish Encyclopedia, online reference, Jewishencyclopedia.com

Kodell Jerome, O.S.B. 1991. *The Eucharist in the New Testament*, Liturgical Press, Collegeville, MN

Knox Ronald, 1948, *The Mass in Slow Motion*, Sheed & Ward, New York, NY

Liturgy of St James, On the Rite of Communion

Lumen Gentium, 1964, *The Constitution on the Catholic Church*, Second Vatican Council, Vatican City

Madrid Patrick, 2002, *Why is That in Tradition?,* Our Sunday Visitor, Huntington, IN

Mazza Enrico, 1999, *The Celebration of the Eucharist: The Origin of the Rite and the Development of Its Interpretation*, Pueblo, Collegeville, MN

McBride Alfred, O Praem, 2006, *A Short History of the Mass*, St. Anthony Messenger Press, Cincinnati, OH

Meagher James L., 1906, *How Christ Said The First Mass*, Christian Press Association Publishing Company, New York, NY

Merton Thomas, 1956, *The Living Bread,* Farrar, Straus & Cudalhy, New York, NY

Moore Gerard, 2004, *Why The Mass Matters A Guide To Praying The Mass*, Pauline Books & Media, Boston, MA

Newton Richard, 1923, *The Jewish Tabernacle And Its Furniture In Their Typical Teachings*, Biblo Bazaar, New York, NY

Norrington David, 1996, *To Preach or Not To Preach? The Church's Urgent Question*, Paternoster Press, Carlisle, UK

Norwich John Julius, 2005, *The Middle Sea A History Of The Mediterranean*, Vintage Books, New York, NY

Pert Candace PhD, 1999, *Molecules of Emotion The Science Behind Mind-Body Medicine*, Simon & Schuster, New York, NY

Pope John Paul II, *Apostolic Exortation Dies Domini*

Ratzinger Joseph Cardinal, 1986, *Feast of Faith: Approaches to a Theology of the Liturgy*, Translated by Graham Harrison, Ignatius Press, San Francisco, CA

Ratzinger Joseph Cardinal, (Pope Benedict XVI), 2003, *God is Near: The Eucharist, the Heart of Life*, Translated by Henry Taylor, Ignatius Press, San Francisco, CA

Ratzinger Joseph Cardinal, (Pope Benedict XVI), 2000, *The Spirit of the Liturgy*, Translated by John Saward, Ignatius Press, San Francisco, CA

Ratzinger Joseph Cardinal, (Pope Benedict XVI), 2000, *A New Song for the Lord: Faith in Christ and the Liturgy Today.* Crossroad, New York, NY

Raeburn Michael, 1984, *Architecture Of The Western World*, Crescent Books, London, UK

Sacrosanctum Concilium, 1964, *The Constitution on the Sacred Liturgy*, Second Vatican Council, Vatican City

San Juan Catholic Seminars, 1993, *Beginning Apologetics How to Explain and Defend the Catholic Faith*, Farmington, NM

Shaw Roxana, October 9, 2012, *Praying The Rosary Is As Good As Yoga For Your Health*, The Huffington Post Journal

Scharfstein Sol, 2008, *Torah, And Commentary: The Five Books Of Moses, Translation Rabbinic and Contemporary Commentary*, KTAV Publishing House, Jersey City, NJ

St Augustine, *The City Of God*, online version

St Cyril of Jerusalem, *Mystagogical Lecture, online version*

St Hippolytus of Rome, *The Apostolic Tradition*, Translation by Burton Scott Easton (1934) and Gregory Dix (1937) online version

St Cyprian of Carthage, *On The Lord's Prayer, onlive version*

Stravinskas Peter, 2000, *The Bible and the Mass*, Newman House, Mount Pocono, PA

Tansey G. Richard and De La Croix Horst, 1986, Art Throgh The Ages Ancient, Medieval, And Non-European Art, HBJ, San Diego, CA

Tobin Greg, 2005, *Holy Father Pope Benedict XVI Pontiff For A New Era*, Sterling Publishing, New York, NY

Van Dorsen Charles, 1991, *A History of Knowledge Past, Present, and Future, The pivotal events, people, and achievements of world history*, Ballantine Books, New York, NY

Vision of Paul the Apostle, From the Ante-Nicene Fathers, Vol X, no 41, Quoted by the Gnostic Society Library Online

Viola Frank, and Barna George, 2008, *Pagan Christianity*, Tyndale House Publishers, Carol Stream, IL

Wegman Herman, 1967, *Christian Worship In The East And West, A Study Guide To Liturgical History*, Pueblo Publishing, New York, NY

Zanolini Antonio, 1923, *Disputationes Ad Sacram Scripturam Spectantis de Festis et Sectis Judaeorum,* Nabu Press, Romani

INDEX

A

B

C

M

N

O

P

Q

T

Z

Nave Illustration: The Origin Of Our Rituals

Sanctuary Illustration: The Origin Of Our Rituals

ABOUT THE AUTHOR

ERICK SANDSTAD also known by many as former Brother Erick, studied in Rome at the Pontifical University Regina Apostolorum where he acquired a Licentiate Degree in Philosophy. He was a Religious Brother for 14 years residing in Salamanca Spain, Hamden, Connecticut and Rome Italy. He holds a Masters Degree in Psychology from Northeastern University in Boston. Erick when not writing, or speaking at events he is helping churches raise capital for new building acquisitions or supporting a diocese with their vocation efforts. He resides in Lexington, Kentucky. For more information please contact him at: ericksandstad@Gmail.com

ACKNOWLEDGEMENTS

No author ever writes a book alone. It would be difficult to acknowledge everyone who contributed to my formation in Rome and Salamanca, Spain. I want to thank in a special way the following people who contributed to the design, layout, illustrations, managing graphics, editing, inspiration, and the many prayers: Laura McKenna Miller, Lauren McKenna Miller, Tove Muller, LuAnn Hamon, Diana Stanciulescu, Ioan Man, Tiffany Pauley, Richard Farrell, Ana Moura, Lea Ann Miller, Catesby and Biz Clay, Najla Lataif, Thor and Monica Sandstad, Heidy and Stella Sandstad and my dear mother, Reyna. Thank you, I love you all.

-ERICK SANDSTAD